1

More
Grammar
Practice

HEINLE & HEINLE

THOMSON LEARNING

United States • Australia • Canada • Mexico • Singapore • Spain • United Kingdom

Contents

PRACTICE 1   Forms and Uses of *Be*

FORMS OF *BE*			USES OF *BE*
I	*am*	in New York now.	*Location*
He		a mechanic.	*Classification*
She		from Canada.	*Place of origin*
Boston	*is*	a city.	*Definition*
It		hot today.	*Weather*
It		6:30.	*Time*
We		at school.	*Location*
You	*are*	six years old.	*Age*
They		big.	*Description*

LANGUAGE NOTE: Use the verb *be* for the following: location, classification, place of origin, definition, weather, time, age, or other description.

EXERCISE 1 Write the correct form of *be* in the sentences below.

Example: He _____ *is* _____ a painter.

1. I _____ a student.
2. I _____ 20 years old.
3. My father _____ a businessman.
4. He _____ always busy.
5. My mother _____ a teacher.
6. She _____ intelligent.
7. New York _____ exciting.
8. It _____ cold in the winter.
9. What time is it? It _____ 5:15.
10. We _____ in Mexico.
11. You _____ my friend.
12. You _____ tall.
13. Dogs _____ animals.
14. Italy and Spain _____ countries.
15. They _____ from Japan.
16. I _____ at school.
17. You _____ at work.
18. He _____ in his room.
19. My sister _____ a doctor.
20. My brother _____ in Boston.
21. They _____ children.
22. Dogs and cats _____ good pets.
23. She _____ funny.
24. I _____ from China.
25. The birds _____ in the trees.
26. My mother _____ beautiful.
27. He _____ my best friend.
28. They _____ roommates.

EXERCISE **2** Circle the correct sentence.

Example: China in Asia. / (China is in Asia.)

1. You happy. / You are happy.

2. I is friendly. / I am friendly.

3. January and February are cold. / January and February am cold.

4. It is hot today. / It are hot today.

5. My mother from Chicago. / My mother is from Chicago.

6. They are from Mexico. / They is from Mexico.

7. It be 4:45 p.m. / It is 4:45 p.m.

8. He am 25 years old. / He is 25 years old.

9. A fly is an insect. / A fly are an insect.

10. She be my sister. / She is my sister.

11. Dr. Jones a dentist. / Dr. Jones is a dentist.

12. She am at work. / She is at work.

12. You is 25 years old. / You are 25 years old.

14. We is at the hospital right now. / We are at the hospital right now.

15. Jill and James are at work. / Jill and James is at work.

16. It is lunchtime. / It lunchtime.

17. Brazil is a beautiful country. / Brazil are a beautiful country.

18. The car in the parking lot. / The car is in the parking lot.

19. They are very sad. / They is very sad.

20. I am a driving teacher. / I is a driving teacher.

EXERCISE **3** Fill in the blanks to make true statements.

Example: (place of origin) We are from _____*Indonesia*_____ .

1. (time) It is _____ now.

2. (weather) It is _____ .

3. (place of origin) I am from

_____ .

4. (location) I am in / at

_____ .

5. (description) I am

_____ .

PRACTICE 2 Subject Pronouns

<u>Chicago</u> is very big.	<u>My friend and I</u> are in California.
▼	▼
It is in Illinois.	**We** are in Los Angeles.
<u>My sister</u> is married.	<u>My cousins</u> are in Mexico.
▼	▼
She is very happy.	**They** are in Mexico City.
<u>My father</u> is at work.	<u>China and Korea</u> are countries.
▼	▼
He is busy.	**They** are in Asia.

LANGUAGE NOTES:
   1. The subject pronouns are *I, you, we, they, he, she,* and *it.*
   2. Subject pronouns can take the place of the subject noun.

EXERCISE 1 Fill in the blanks with the correct pronoun.

Example: Daniel and Yoshio are students. *They* _____ are students.

1. <u>The pencil</u> is lost. _____ is lost.

2. <u>Julie</u> is a doctor. _____ is a doctor.

3. <u>The mother</u> is asleep. _____ is asleep.

4. <u>The father</u> is in his room. _____ is in his room.

5. <u>My brother and I</u> like sports. _____ like sports.

6. <u>My cousins</u> are in Mexico. _____ are in Mexico.

7. <u>Amy</u> is my favorite singer. _____ is my favorite singer.

8. <u>Joshua</u> is a hard worker. _____ is a hard worker.

9. <u>Karen and Lisa</u> are my best friends. _____ are my best friends.

10. <u>Tom and Paul</u> aren't friends. _____ aren't friends.

11. <u>Donald</u> is my teacher. _____ is my teacher.

12. <u>Bombay</u> is in India. _____ is in India.

13. <u>Carrots and potatoes</u> are vegetables. _____ are healthy foods.

14. <u>You and I</u> are so happy together. _____ are so happy together.

15. <u>Maria</u> is a dancer. _____ is a dancer.

16. <u>Your English</u> is very good. _____ is very good.

17. <u>I</u> am tired. _____ am sleepy.

18. Tim and Allen are brothers. _____ are brothers.

19. My uncle is on vacation in Hawaii. _____ is on vacation in Hawaii.

20. The cat and the dog are good friends. _____ are good friends.

21. My mother is a teacher. _____ is a teacher.

22. You and I are from the same school. _____ are from the same school.

23. English is a difficult language. _____ is a difficult language.

24. France and Italy are countries. _____ are countries.

25. Rome is a city. _____ is in Italy.

EXERCISE 2 Circle the correct answer.

Example: He / (We) are good friends.

1. It / She is cold and rainy today.
2. They / I am in the house right now.
3. They / He are at home with me.
4. We / It is time for dinner.
5. It / She is a city in Europe.
6. It / We are on vacation.
7. It / You is really interesting.
8. We / They are big countries.
9. You / He is my best friend.
10. They / It are my favorite colors.

11. They / It is delicious.
12. He / They are in the same class.
13. I / You am a student.
14. He / It is about 4:00 a.m.
15. We / He are cousins.
16. She / You is a doctor.
17. We / They are difficult languages.
18. It / He is a big city.
19. You / He are at work.
20. They / She is interesting.

EXERCISE 3 Write the correct form of *be* after each subject pronoun.

Example: We _____*are*_____ on a trip to New York City.

1. They _____ in Australia.
2. He _____ a teacher.
3. I _____ from Argentina.
4. It _____ a small school.

5. It _____ stormy today.
6. You _____ at home.
7. She _____ 25 years old.
8. We _____ from China.

Practice 2 **7**

PRACTICE 3   Contractions with *Be*

FULL FORM	CONTRACTION	EXPLANATION
I am	**I'm** in New York City.	A contraction is a short form of a subject or subject pronoun + *am*, *is*, or *are*.
You are	**You're** at home.	
It is	**It's** beautiful.	
She is	**She's** happy.	
He is	**He's** busy.	
We are	**We're** tired.	
They are	**They're** on vacation.	
My daughter is	**My daughter's** with me.	We can make a contraction with most nouns and *is*.
New York is	**New York's** busy.	
Traffic is	**Traffic's** terrible.	
My husband is	**My husband's** at home.	

LANGUAGE NOTES:

1. Use contractions in spoken language and informal writing.
2. Don't make contractions with *is* with nouns that end in the sounds *s*, *z*, *sh*, or *ch*:
    France **is** in Europe.
3. Don't make contractions with a plural noun and *are:*
    The trees **are** beautiful.

EXERCISE 1   Rewrite these sentences using contractions. If a contraction is not possible, do not rewrite the sentence.

Examples: They are at school.   *They're at school.*

   The church is big.   _____

1.   I am happy.   _____

2.   We are at home.   _____

3.   School is interesting.   _____

4.   English is easy.   _____

5.   He is tired.   _____

6.   It is a nice day today.   _____

7.   My name is Junko.   _____

8.   My house is big.   _____

9.   You are nice.   _____

10.   She is my sister.   _____

EXERCISE 2 Fill in the blanks with the correct form of *be*. Make a contraction whenever possible. Not every sentence can have a contraction.

Example: Jackie *'s* _____ busy today.

The girls _____ *are* _____ on vacation.

1. George and Michael _____ brothers. They live in Florida.

2. Florida _____ a warm state in the United States. It _____ in the south.

3. Their house _____ near the beach. It _____ a big house with a swimming pool.

4. George and his father _____ tall. Michael _____ not so tall.

5. Maurice _____ their father's name. He _____ a writer.

6. This _____ their dog, Pooch. Pooch _____ very small.

7. Pooch _____ a good swimmer. She _____ always happy.

8. Maurice _____ a good swimmer too.

9. Pooch and Maurice _____ in the pool now.

10. Michael and Jackie _____ in the kitchen.

EXERCISE 3 Fill in the blanks with a form of *be*. Make a contraction whenever possible. Not every sentence can have a contraction.

Dear Yumiko,

I _____ *'m* _____ in New York City now. It _____ very exciting. It
     (1)   (2)

_____ a very big, beautiful city. There _____ so many tall
     (3)   (4)

buildings and fashionable people. I think New York _____ the most important city
                                                        (5)

in the world. English _____ the main language of New York, but I hear people
                        (6)

speaking many other languages too. Chinese and Spanish _____ very common. I
                                                              (7)

_____ a student of English at a small language school. The school
     (8)

_____ on a busy street. The students _____ from many countries.
     (9)   (10)

The teachers _____ strict, but funny. A big restaurant _____
                 (11)   (12)

near the school. The food _____ delicious. Everything _____ new
                             (13)   (14)

and exciting for me here. I hope you can come visit soon.

Your friend, Reiko

Practice 3   **9**

PRACTICE 4 *Be* with Location and Origin

PREPOSITION	EXAMPLE
on	The book is **on** the table.
at (a general area)	I am **at** school.
in (a complete or partial enclosure)	The students are **in** the classroom.
in front of	The teacher is **in front of** the students.
in back of / behind	The chalkboard is **in back of** / **behind** the desk.
between	The empty desk is **between** the two students.
over / above	The exit sign is **over** / **above** the door.
below / under	The textbooks are **below** / **under** the desk.
near / by / close to	The sharpener is **near** / **by** / **close to** the window.
next to	The light switch is **next to** the door.
far from	Spain is **far from** India.
across from	Room 202 is **across from** Room 203.
in (a city)	The White House is **in** Washington, D.C.
on (a street)	The White House is **on** Pennsylvania Avenue.
at (an address)	The White House is **at** 1600 Pennsylvania Avenue.
from	Mario is **from** Brazil.

LANGUAGE NOTES:

1. We use prepositions to show location and origin.
2. Word order = subject + *be* + preposition + place.

EXERCISE 1 Circle the correct preposition for each sentence.

Example: I live (on) / from the top floor of my building.

1. My mother is in / at San Francisco.

2. Her apartment house is on / between Fulton Street.

3. It is on / at 543 Fulton Street.

4. She lives in / on the first floor.

5. My mother is from / under Sweden.

6. There is a lot of snow at / in Sweden in the winter.

7. Stockholm is in / on Sweden.

8. Brazil is in / at South America.

9. Sweden is next to / far from Mexico.

10. My best friend is <u>by / from</u> Iran.

11. Iran is <u>under / between</u> Afghanistan and Iraq.

12. She is standing <u>over / between</u> her mother and her father in the photo.

13. A tall man is <u>in front of / at</u> me.

14. The sun is <u>behind / at</u> the clouds.

15. The doctor is <u>over / at</u> the hospital.

16. Dinner is <u>under / on</u> the table.

17. Our feet are <u>over / under</u> the table at dinnertime.

18. The park is <u>under / across from</u> my house.

19. The light is <u>next to / between</u> my bed.

20. The fish are <u>close to / in</u> the ocean.

EXERCISE 2 Use a form of *be* and a preposition to tell the location of these people and things.

Example: My coat *is in the closet.* _____

1. My town _____

2. My house _____

3. My room _____

4. My books _____

5. My bed _____

6. The light switch _____

7. The television _____

8. The wastebasket _____

9. My desk _____

10. I _____

11. My friend _____

12. My teacher _____

13. My school _____

14. My family _____

PRACTICE 5 — *This, That, These,* and *Those*

	NEAR	NOT NEAR / FAR
Singular	**This** is my school.	**That** is my teacher.
Plural	**These** are my books.	**Those** are tall buildings.

LANGUAGE NOTES:

1. We use *this, that, these,* and *those* to identify objects and people.
2. Only *that + is* can form a contraction in writing: *that's.*
3. Use *this, that, these,* or *those* alone or with a noun following it:
   Those are my friends.
   Those friends are funny.

EXERCISE 1 Read each sentence. Then identify whether the subject of the sentence is singular or plural.

Example: Do you like this hat? _____*singular*_____

1. These shoes hurt! _____
2. Bring me that book. _____
3. Those are my pens. _____
4. This is my sister, Juanita. _____
5. Those sandwiches are delicious. _____
6. This is my favorite CD. _____
7. My friend gave me that painting. _____
8. Is this your computer? _____
9. I hope you like these gifts. _____
10. That movie is wonderful. _____

EXERCISE 2 Read each sentence. Then identify whether the subject of the sentence is *near* or *far* from the speaker.

Example: Do you like these shoes? _____*near*_____

1. That ring is beautiful. _____
2. Those boys are in the soccer game. _____
3. This telephone is broken. _____
4. These student tests are excellent. _____
5. Is that man your father? _____
6. Are these books library books? _____

7. Is <u>this</u> your answer to my question? _____

8. <u>Those dishes</u> are dirty. _____

9. Are <u>those people</u> in your class? _____

10. Are <u>these</u> ready to be washed? _____

EXERCISE 3 Fill in the blanks with *this, that, these,* or *those* and the appropriate form of *be* to complete the sentence. The arrows will tell you if the object or person is near or far.

Examples: *This is* _____ my bag. ⟶

Those are _____ my shoes. ⟶⟶⟶

1. _____ a great movie. ⟶⟶⟶

2. _____ delicious strawberries. ⟶⟶⟶⟶

3. _____ your socks. ⟶

4. _____ expensive clothes. ⟶⟶⟶

5. _____ an interesting book. ⟶

6. _____ useful notes. ⟶

7. _____ my favorite color. ⟶⟶⟶

8. _____ my notebook. ⟶

9. _____ your car. ⟶⟶⟶

10. _____ beautiful flowers. ⟶⟶⟶

11. _____ big clouds. ⟶⟶⟶

12. _____ new pants. ⟶

13. _____ a good company. ⟶⟶⟶

14. _____ an old song. ⟶

15. _____ a funny joke. ⟶⟶⟶

16. _____ nice gloves. ⟶⟶⟶

17. _____ a useful exercise. ⟶

18. _____ paperclips. ⟶

19. _____ a fashionable hat. ⟶⟶⟶

20. _____ my boyfriend, Mike. ⟶

PRACTICE 6 Negative Statements with *Be*

EXAMPLE	EXPLANATION
I am **not** married. Peter is **not** at home. We are **not** doctors.	We put *not* after a form of *be* to make a negative statement.
I'm not late. English **isn't** my native language. My friends **aren't** here now.	We can make contractions in negative statements.

LANGUAGE NOTE:

There is only one contraction of *I am not*. There are two negative contractions for all other combinations. Study the negative contractions.

Negative Contractions with *Be*

I am not	I'm not	—
you are not	you're not	you aren't
he is not	he's not	he isn't
she is not	she's not	she isn't
it is not	it's not	it isn't
we are not	we're not	we aren't
they are not	they're not	they aren't

EXERCISE 1 Fill in the blanks with a pronoun and a negative verb. Practice using both negative forms.

Example: Mary is a doctor.

    Mary isn't _____ a nurse.

    Mary's not _____ a teacher.

1. He's from Canada.

    _____ from the United States.

    _____ from England.

2. She's in the house.

    _____ at work.

    _____ in school.

3. My parents are in India.

    _____ in Hawaii.

    _____ here.

4. This is a computer.

   _____ a television.

   _____ a radio.

5. You're late.

   _____ on time.

   _____ early.

6. We are in class.

   _____ at the movies.

   _____ at a restaurant.

7. I am cold.

   _____ hot.

   _____ warm.

8. My brother is short and thin.

   _____ tall.

   _____ heavy.

EXERCISE 2 Fill in the blanks with a form of *be* to make a true affirmative or negative statement.

Example: Kuala Lumpur _____*is*_____ in Malaysia.

1. I _____ a pilot.

2. I _____ a student.

3. You _____ late.

4. The trees _____ green.

5. Africa _____ a city.

6. India _____ a state.

7. Beijing _____ in Japan.

8. Tokyo _____ in Japan.

9. China _____ small.

10. Mexico City _____ a country.

PRACTICE 7 — *Be* in *Yes / No* Questions and Short Answers

YES / NO QUESTION	SHORT ANSWER
Am I a good student?	**Yes, you are.**
Are you from Paris?	**No, I'm not.**
Is he absent?	**No, he isn't.**
Is she happy?	**Yes, she is.**
Is it windy?	**Yes, it is.**
Are we late?	**No, you aren't.**
Are they from Mexico?	**Yes, they are.**

LANGUAGE NOTES:

1. To ask a *yes / no* question with the verb *be*, put a form of *be* before the subject.
2. We don't use a contraction for a short *yes* answer:
   Yes, *it is.* [**not:** Yes, *it's.*]
3. We usually use a contraction for a short *no* answer.
   No, it isn't. **or** No, it's not.

EXERCISE 1 Change the following sentences to questions. Keep the same subject.

Example: He is a student. *Is he a student?*

1. She is a teacher. _____
2. Dean is in Africa. _____
3. We are sad today. _____
4. They are in business. _____
5. It is foggy right now. _____
6. I am an artist. _____
7. You are a good friend. _____
8. He is honest and kind. _____
9. Mrs. Williams is pleased. _____
10. Mr. Hart is at home. _____
11. We are in an expensive restaurant. _____
12. It is almost dinnertime. _____
13. You are excited to be here. _____
14. I am alone today. _____
15. They are hungry. _____

EXERCISE 2 Write questions with the words given. Then write a short answer.

Example: children / quiet *Are children quiet?*
No, they aren't.

1. diamonds / cheap _____

   _____

2. ice cream / healthy _____

   _____

3. cats / good pets _____

   _____

4. English / interesting _____

   _____

5. cars / necessary _____

   _____

6. food / free _____

   _____

7. computers / useful _____

   _____

8. pencils / expensive _____

   _____

EXERCISE 3 Answer the following questions. Give the correct answer if you write *no*.

Example: Are you a teacher? *No, I'm not. I'm a student.*

1. Are you a student? _____

2. Are you from the United States? _____

3. Are you married? _____

4. Is English hard for you? _____

5. Are you tired? _____

6. Are you hungry? _____

7. Is your family big? _____

8. Is it cold today? _____

PRACTICE 8 — *Wh–* Questions

QUESTION WORD	QUESTION	ANSWER
Who = person	**Who** is your teacher?	My teacher is Ms. Weiss.
What = thing	**What** is your name?	My name is Linda.
	What is a giraffe?	A giraffe is an animal.
When = time Use *on* for days and dates. Use *in* for months and years.	**When** is Christmas? **When** is your birthday?	It's on December 25. It's in June.
Why = reason	**Why** is Mr. Park absent?	He's absent because he's sick.
Where = place	**Where** is China?	It's in Asia.
How = description, health	**How** is the weather today? **How** is your mother?	It's warm today. She's fine.

LANGUAGE NOTES:
1. A *wh–* question asks for information.
2. The *wh–* word + *is* can form a contraction:
   Where's your father?
   How's the job?

EXERCISE 1 Fill in the blanks with the correct question word.

Example: _What_____ is your name? My name is Lee.

1. _____ is Seoul? — It's in Korea.
2. _____ is your birthday? — It's in January.
3. _____ is your favorite singer? — My favorite singer is Madonna.
4. _____ is a horse? — A horse is an animal.
5. _____ are you late? — I'm late because I missed the train.
6. _____ are your shoes? — They are outside.
7. _____ is your sister? — She's fine, thanks.
8. _____ is your homework? — It's in my bag.
9. _____ is New Year's Eve? — It's on December 31.
10. _____ are my books? — They're on your desk.
11. _____ is he so tired? — He is tired because he is so busy.
12. _____ is in your refrigerator? — Some fruit and vegetables are in there.

13. _____ is in your English class?   Some good students are in my class.

14. _____ are we right now?   You are in your classroom.

15. _____ is the homework?   The homework is a composition.

EXERCISE 2 Turn these statements into questions.

Example: *What is a rose?*   A rose is a flower.

1. _____   Red is a color.

2. _____   My birthday is in February.

3. _____   Life in New York is exciting.

4. _____   Vietnam is in Asia.

5. _____   He's from Turkey.

6. _____   My teacher is Ms. Sands.

7. _____   It's cold today.

8. _____   She's smart because she studies hard.

9. _____   I'm fine, thanks.

10. _____   My pens are on my desk.

11. _____   My name is Maria.

12. _____   His birthday is on July 3.

EXERCISE 3 Complete the questions. Then write true answers to the questions.

Example: *Who is* _____ your favorite painter?   *My favorite painter is Picasso.*

1. _____ your teacher?   _____

2. _____ your best friend?   _____

3. _____ your name?   _____

4. _____ your birthday?   _____

5. _____ you study English?   _____

6. _____ you from?   _____

7. _____ you now?   _____

8. _____ the weather today?   _____

PRACTICE 9 Forms and Uses of the Simple Present Tense

SUBJECT	BASE FORM	COMPLEMENT	SUBJECT	–S FORM	COMPLEMENT
I			He		
You			She		
We	**need**	water.	It	**needs**	water.
They			A plant		
Trees			A person		

EXAMPLE	USE
Cats **like** milk.	With general truths
Japanese people **bow** when they meet.	With customs
We **take** a vacation every summer.	To show regular or repeated actions or habits
He **comes** from Iraq.	To show places of origin

LANGUAGE NOTE:
Three verbs have an irregular –s form: *have / has, go / goes,* and *do / does.*

EXERCISE 1   Write the correct verb in each of the sentences below.

Example: George and Mary (need / needs) _____ *need* _____ a new house.

1. Carlos (like / likes) _____ ice cream.

2. Tomoko (want / wants) _____ a new bicycle.

3. Many people (think / thinks) _____ it's good.

4. I (hate / hates) _____ parties.

5. They (go / goes) _____ to school on Saturdays.

6. Julia (come / comes) _____ from England.

7. Birds (fly / flies) _____ in the sky.

8. New York (have / has) _____ many tall buildings.

9. He (write / writes) _____ novels.

10. My family (watch / watches) _____ a lot of TV.

11. You (does / do) _____ your homework every night.

12. I (go / goes) _____ to exercise after school.

13. Sherrie (eat / eats) _____ lunch before our class.

14. We (laugh / laughs) _____ at her jokes.

15. They (visit / visits) _____ their family in Morocco.

16. Jane and Sandra (wants / want) _____ to travel a lot.

EXERCISE 2 Read each sentence below, and label it *truth, custom, habit,* or *origin.*

Example: I bite my fingernails. _____*habit*_____

1. Marilyn comes from New Zealand. _____

2. Japan has many temples. _____

3. He eats his bread with butter. _____

4. French people go on vacation in August. _____

5. Noodles come from China. _____

6. Food costs money. _____

7. I go to the movies on weekends. _____

8. They play tennis together. _____

9. My teacher speaks English. _____

10. I come from Peru. _____

EXERCISE 3 Write the correct form of the verb. Then finish the sentence with your own ideas.

Example: He (like) *likes our English class.* _____

1. I (live) _____

2. My family (live) _____

3. I (study) _____

4. My school (have) _____

5. My teacher (speak) _____

6. The students in my class (do) _____

7. Our classroom (have) _____

8. I (read) _____

9. My friend (read) _____

10. I (like) _____

11. My friend (want) _____

12. My family (go) _____

PRACTICE 10 Negative Statements with the Simple Present Tense

EXAMPLE	EXPLANATION
Sara **lives** in Washington. Sara **doesn't live** in Chicago. She **doesn't live** in San Francisco.	Use *doesn't* + the base form with *he, she, it,* or a singular noun.
Her parents **live** in Chicago. Her parents **don't live** in Washington. They **don't live** in San Francisco.	Use *don't* + the base form with *I, you, we, they,* or a plural noun.

LANGUAGE NOTES:

1. *Don't* is the contraction for *do not. Doesn't* is the contraction for *does not.*
2. Always use the base form after *don't* and *doesn't.*

EXERCISE 1 Fill in the blanks with the negative form of the underlined verb.

Example: My cousin Danielle <u>lives</u> in London.

       She _____*doesn't live*_____ in San Francisco.

1. My cousin Danielle <u>comes</u> from England. She _____ from the United States.
2. She <u>lives</u> alone in London. She _____ with her parents.
3. Her parents <u>live</u> in Hastings. They _____ in London.
4. She <u>works</u> in London. She _____ in New York.
5. She <u>has</u> a lot of work. She _____ much free time.
6. Danielle <u>likes</u> classical music. She _____ popular music as much.
7. On weekends, Danielle <u>goes</u> to concerts. She _____ to discos.
8. Danielle <u>works</u> as a teacher. She _____ as a secretary.
9. She <u>eats</u> a lot of vegetables. She _____ meat.
10. She <u>wears</u> colorful clothes. She _____ black clothes.

EXERCISE 2 Rewrite the sentence using the affirmative form of the underlined verb.

Example: I <u>don't know</u> how to speak French. (She) *She knows how to speak French.*

1. You <u>don't work</u> every day. (I) _____
2. I <u>don't understand</u> English well. (You) _____
3. He <u>doesn't play</u> basketball. (She) _____
4. She <u>doesn't ride</u> a motorcycle. (They) _____

5. We <u>don't read</u> at night. (She) _____

6. You <u>don't like</u> vegetables. (I) _____

7. They <u>don't seem</u> happy. (He) _____

8. She <u>doesn't write</u> e-mails to us. (You) _____

9. It <u>doesn't work</u> well. (We) _____

10. I <u>don't add</u> correctly. (It) _____

EXERCISE 3 Tell if your hometown *has* or *doesn't have* the following features.

Example: (a library) My hometown *doesn't have a library.* _____

1. (a movie theater) My hometown _____

2. (a farm) My hometown _____

3. (a university) My hometown _____

4. (a museum) My hometown _____

5. (clean air) My hometown _____

6. (tall buildings) My hometown _____

EXERCISE 4 Write affirmative or negative true statements about yourself.

Example: (speak French) *I don't speak French.* _____

1. (like sports) _____

2. (have a dog) _____

3. (eat breakfast every day) _____

4. (have a bicycle) _____

5. (like hot weather) _____

6. (speak Russian) _____

7. (have a job) _____

8. (go to discos) _____

9. (draw pictures) _____

10. (watch TV every night) _____

11. (stay up until midnight) _____

12. (call my family every week) _____

Negative Statements with the Simple Present Tense

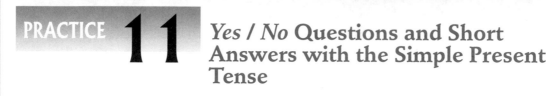

PRACTICE 11 — Yes / No Questions and Short Answers with the Simple Present Tense

EXAMPLE	EXPLANATION
Does Sara **live** in Washington? Yes, she **does**.	We use *do* or *does* to form a *yes / no* question. We always use the base form after *do* or *does*.
Do her parents **live** in Washington? No, they **don't**.	We can answer with a short answer.

DO / DOES	SUBJECT	VERB	COMPLEMENT	SHORT ANSWER
	Tourists	visit	the White House.	
Do	they	visit	the president's private rooms?	No, they don't.
	The president	lives	in the White House.	
Does	the vice president	live	in the White House?	No, he doesn't.

LANGUAGE NOTES:

1. Use *does* with *he, she, it,* and singular subjects.
2. Use *do* with *I, you, we, they,* and plural subjects.
3. We usually answer a *yes / no* question with a short answer.
4. The short answer uses a pronoun.
5. The short answer uses a contraction in the negative.

EXERCISE 1 Read each statement. Then write a *yes / no* question using that statement. Change the subject to a pronoun.

Examples: Joseph has a notebook. *Does he have a notebook?*

We enjoy music. *Do we enjoy music?*

1. My mother reads the newspaper every day.

   _____

2. We study English grammar.

   _____

3. The teacher gives us homework.

   _____

4. The school has classrooms.

   _____

5. You drink water at break time.

   _____

6. The man speaks English in his job.

   _____

7. The students use cell phones at break time.

   _____

8. The director orders new books for the school.

   _____

EXERCISE 2 Write answers to the questions below.

Example: Do you live in Turkey? _Yes, I do._____ **or** _No, I don't._____

1. Do you like English? _____
2. Do you have a pet? _____
3. Does your mother work? _____
4. Do you eat breakfast every day? _____
5. Do you live with your parents? _____
6. Do you like fish? _____
7. Do you eat meat? _____
8. Does your school have computers? _____

EXERCISE 3 Two friends are comparing jobs. Fill in the blanks to complete this conversation.

Example: Do you _____ _read_ _____ at work?

A: Do you (1) _____ your new job?

B: No, (2) _____. I have a very strict boss. I'm always busy.

A: (3) _____ take breaks?

B: No, (4) _____. I take only a lunch break. Also, I have to work on Saturdays. (5) _____ on Saturdays?

A: No, never! I work only on weekdays.

B: (6) _____ you _____ after five o'clock?

A: Yes, (7) _____. I work late every day. Do you work late?

B: No, (8) _____. I like to go home at five o'clock.

PRACTICE 12 Comparing *Yes / No* Questions with *Be* and Other Verbs

Are you lost? No, I'm not.	Am I right? Yes, you are.
Do you need help? No, I don't.	Do I have the right answer? Yes, you do
Are they from Haiti? Yes, they are.	Is the teacher British? No, he isn't.
Do they speak French? Yes, they do.	Does he have an accent? No, he doesn't

LANGUAGE NOTE:

Use *be* in short answers when the question contains *be*. Use *do* or *does* in short answers with all other present tense verbs.

EXERCISE 1 Write a positive and a negative short answer for each question.

Examples: Do you study a lot?   *Yes, I do.*   *No, I don't.*

          Are you busy tonight?   *Yes, I am.*   *No, I'm not.*

1.   Do you like pizza for dinner?   _____   _____

2.   Do we leave at eight o'clock?   _____   _____

3.   Do they know their neighbor?   _____   _____

4.   Does she work at the library?   _____   _____

5.   Do I like all of my friends?   _____   _____

6.   Are you content at this school?   _____   _____

7.   Are we correct in our answer?   _____   _____

8.   Are they together at the café?   _____   _____

9.   Is he from Mexico?   _____   _____

10.   Is she an engineer?   _____   _____

11.   Is the pen in the notebook?   _____   _____

12.   Am I worried about the test?   _____   _____

EXERCISE 2 All of these are questions. Put the words in the correct order. End each question with a question mark (?).

Example: Australians / English / speak / do   *Do Australians speak English?*

1.   Russia / a big country / is   _____

2.   Mexicans / Spanish / speak / do   _____

3.   do / know / you / college math   _____

4.   the Earth / very large / is   _____

5.   your friends / does / visit / she   _____

Read each statement. Then write a *yes / no* question about the words in parentheses ( ). Write or finish the short answer.

Example: China is a big country.

(England)   *Is England a big country?*

Answer: *No, it isn't.*

1.   Indonesia is a warm country.

(Iceland)   _____

Answer: No, _____

2.   French people eat a lot of cheese.

(Japanese people)   _____

Answer: No, _____

3.   Trains in Tokyo run on time.

(trains in your city)   _____

Answer: Yes, _____

4.   Mexican food is spicy.

(Korean food)   _____

Answer: Yes, _____

5.   Brazilians speak Portuguese.

(Argentineans)   _____

Answer: No, _____

6.   Soccer is popular in Japan.

(baseball)   _____

Answer: Yes, _____

7.   You study grammar.

(history)   _____

Answer: Yes, _____

Comparing *Yes / No* Questions with *Be* and Other Verbs

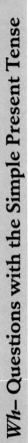
PRACTICE 13 Wh– Questions with the Simple Present Tense

WH–WORD	DO / DOES DON'T / DOESN'T	SUBJECT	VERB	COMPLEMENT	SHORT ANSWER
		My brother	**works**	in Washington.	
	Does	he	**work**	for the government?	No, he **doesn't.**
Where	does	he	**work?**		
Why	doesn't	he	**work**	for the government?	
		They	**have**	a car.	
	Do	they	**have**	an American car?	Yes, they **do.**

LANGUAGE NOTE: The correct word order for *wh*– questions is *wh*– word + *do / does / don't / doesn't* + subject + base form of verb + complement + ?

EXERCISE 1 Fill in the blanks with the missing words.

Example: Why _____*do*_____ you want to learn English?

1. When _____ you do your homework?
2. Where _____ she go on vacation each year?
3. _____ do you live?
4. Where _____ he work?
5. How many children _____ she have?
6. Why _____ they always come to school together?
7. Why _____ you practice your English more often?
8. How often _____ you brush your teeth?
9. What time _____ you wake up?
10. _____ does she eat lunch with?

EXERCISE 2 Create *wh*– questions for the following underlined answers.

Example:

Q: *Where do you go to school?*

A: I go to school in London.

1. **Q:** _____

   A: I go shopping at Macy's.

28 Practice 13

2. **Q:** _____

    A: She spends the weekends <u>with her family.</u>

3. **Q:** _____

    A: I study <u>at my friend's house.</u>

4. **Q:** _____

    A: They have <u>two</u> dogs.

5. **Q:** _____

    A: My uncle lives <u>in Argentina.</u>

6. **Q:** _____

    A: I call my mother <u>twice a week.</u>

7. **Q:** _____

    A: We jog every day <u>because we enjoy it.</u>

8. **Q:** _____

    A: They speak <u>Italian.</u>

EXERCISE 3   Unscramble the words below to form questions.

Example: you / do / in the morning / what / eat

    What do you eat in the morning? _____

1. does / when / letters / write / he

   _____

2. she / does / go / after school / where

   _____

3. do / when / English / practice / you

   _____

4. how often / your friends / e-mail / you / do

   _____

5. is / who / film actor / your favorite

   _____

6. want / you / to leave / do / when

   _____

PRACTICE 14 — Wh– Questions with Prepositions

WH– WORD	DO / DOES	SUBJECT	VERB (BASE FORM)	(PREPOSITION)
Where	does	your friend	come	from?
What floor	do	you	live	on?

LANGUAGE NOTES:

1. In formal writing, we put the preposition before a question word. In conversation, we usually put the preposition at the end of the question:
   Formal: On what floor do you live?
   Informal: What floor do you live *on?*
2. We use *whom* after a preposition. We often use *who* when the preposition is at the end:
   Formal: With *whom* do you live?
   Informal: *Who* do you live with?

EXERCISE 1 Label each sentence *formal* or *informal.*

Example: To whom do you speak every day? _____ *formal* _____

1. What bus do you ride on? _____
2. On which train do you travel? _____
3. Who do you go to for help? _____
4. About whom do you think? _____
5. What does he look at every day? _____
6. At what station does he wait? _____

EXERCISE 2 Unscramble the words below to form questions and add question marks.

Example: you / from / come / where / do   *Where do you come from?* _____

1. kind of music / what / do / you / listen to _____
2. you / what / do / eat / in the morning _____
3. where / he / sleep / at night / does _____
4. with / work / who / you / do _____
5. over / why / come / he / doesn't _____
6. do / who / you / with / talk _____
7. she / come / does / where / from _____
8. you / what / do / dream / about _____

EXERCISE 3 Write two questions for the words given. First write a *yes* / *no* question. Then write a *wh*– question.

Example: like ice cream / what flavor

Do you like ice cream?

What flavor do you like?

1. go camping / where

   _____

   _____

2. go to parties / with whom *or* who . . . with

   _____

   _____

3. surf the Internet / with whom *or* who . . . with

   _____

   _____

4. have a car / what kind of

   _____

   _____

5. study English / why

   _____

   _____

EXERCISE 4 Write questions for the answers given below. Use a *wh*– word and a preposition.

Example: *What floor do you live on?*   I live on the second floor.

1. _____ I live with my brother.
2. _____ I come from Australia.
3. _____ I listen to rock music.
4. _____ It goes over the mountain.
5. _____ I think about my job.
6. _____ I'm from Shanghai.
7. _____ He goes to Berkeley College.
8. _____ She waits for Bus 9.

Regular Noun Plurals

WORD ENDING	EXAMPLE WORD	PLURAL ADDITION	PLURAL FORM
Vowel	bee banana	+ s	bees bananas
Consonant	bed month	+ s	beds months
ss, sh, ch, x	class dish church box	+ es	classes dishes churches boxes
Vowel + y	boy monkey	+ s	boys monkeys
Consonant + y	lady party	y changes to ies	ladies parties
Vowel + o	patio stereo	+ s	patios stereos
Consonant + o	mosquito potato	+ es*	mosquitoes potatoes

*Exceptions: photos, pianos, solos, altos, sopranos, autos, avocados.

f or fe	knife calf	f changes to ves**	knives calves

**Exceptions: beliefs, chiefs, roofs, chefs.

EXERCISE 1 Write the plural form of each noun.

Example: lady _____ladies_____

1. ray _____
2. toy _____
3. toe _____
4. kiss _____
5. wish _____
6. fox _____
7. key _____
8. life _____
9. comma _____
10. solo _____
11. couch _____
12. book _____
13. chief _____
14. chef _____
15. knife _____
16. leaf _____

EXERCISE 2 Write the singular form of each noun.

Example: cameras _____*camera*_____

1. radios _____
2. fairies _____
3. ranches _____
4. trees _____
5. dogs _____
6. cans _____
7. paths _____
8. houses _____

9. porches _____
10. stars _____
11. babies _____
12. mosquitoes _____
13. solos _____
14. calves _____
15. glasses _____
16. wives _____

EXERCISE 3 Fill in the blanks with the plural form of the noun given.

Example: We can't eat outside. There are too many (fly) _*flies*_____.

1. Are you going to the store? We need some (potato) _____.
2. How many (lady) _____ are in the room?
3. I have three (radio) _____.
4. There are some (dish) _____ in the cupboard.
5. How many (class) _____ does your school have?
6. They have two (boy) _____ and three
   (girl) _____.
7. Do you have any (box) _____?
8. What are your (month) _____ for school vacation?
9. She loves to take care of (baby) _____.
10. Take out all the (knife) _____ and
    (fork) _____.
11. We love all the (monkey) _____ at the zoo.
12. I always break the (glass) _____.

PRACTICE 16 Irregular Noun Plurals

SINGULAR	PLURAL	EXAMPLE	EXPLANATION
man	men	One **man** is here.	Vowel change
woman	women	Two **men** are there.	
mouse	mice	One **woman** is late.	
tooth	teeth	Five **women** are on time.	
foot	feet		
goose	geese		
sheep	sheep	One **sheep** is here.	No change
fish	fish	Three **sheep** are there.	
deer	deer		
child	children	One **person** is late.	Different word form
person	people (or persons)	Five people are absent.	
	pajamas	Your **clothes** are clean.	No singular form
	clothes		
	pants / slacks		
	(eye) glasses	My **glasses** are broken.	
	scissors		

LANGUAGE NOTES:

1. *People* is more common than *persons:*
   Five *people* in my class speak Spanish.
2. Number words (*hundred, thousand, million*) use the singular form:
   The United States has over 270 million people.
   Two hundred people live in my building.

EXERCISE 1 The following nouns have an irregular plural form. Write the plural form.

Example: woman _____*women*_____

1. tooth _____
2. man _____
3. businesswoman _____
4. person _____
5. sheep _____
6. deer _____
7. foot _____
8. mouse _____
9. child _____
10. fish _____
11. goose _____
12. life _____

EXERCISE 2 The following nouns are shown in irregular plural form. Write the singular form. If there is no singular form, write ø.

Example: deer _____ *deer* _____

slacks _____ *ø* _____

1. chairpeople _____
2. pajamas _____
3. eyeglasses _____
4. children _____
5. geese _____

6. clothes _____
7. feet _____
8. scissors _____
9. pants _____
10. fishermen _____

EXERCISE 3 Fill in the blanks in the following sentences with the plural forms of the nouns given.

Example: Those are nice (pants) *pants* _____.

1. I want some new (clothes) _____.
2. There are three (person) _____ in the room.
3. My (foot) _____ are tired.
4. We saw five (deer) _____ in the forest.
5. We saw a lot of (bird) _____ too.
6. Where are all the (policeman) _____?
7. I have six (watch) _____.
8. Her (tooth) _____ are so white!
9. There are (mouse) _____ and (rat) _____ in this apartment.
10. Look at the (goose) _____ and (duck) _____ on the pond.
11. How many (child) _____ do you have?
12. Do you like (peach) _____?

PRACTICE 17 Using *There + Be*

SINGULAR: *THERE IS* (*+ NOT*)	SINGULAR WORD	SINGULAR NOUN	PREPOSITIONAL PHRASE
There is (There's)	a	janitor	in my building.
There is	one	dryer	in the basement.
There isn't	an	air conditioner	in my apartment.
There is	no	back door	in my apartment.

PLURAL: *THERE ARE* (*+ NOT*)	PLURAL WORD	SINGULAR NOUN	PREPOSITIONAL PHRASE
There are	—	numbers	on the doors of the apartments.
There are	several	windows	in the bedroom.
There are	many	Americans	in my building.
There are	some	children	in my building.
There are	two	closets	in the hall.
There aren't	any	shades	on the windows.
There are	no	shades	on the windows

LANGUAGE NOTES:

1. Use *there + is* to introduce a singular subject into a conversation. Use *there + are* to introduce a plural subject.
2. We can make a contraction for *there is* → *there's*. We don't write a contraction for *there are*.
3. A sentence that begins with *there* often shows a place or a time.
   There's a good movie *at the Garden Theater.*
   There's a good movie *at eight o'clock.*

EXERCISE 1 Use *There is / There are* to complete the following sentences.

Example: _There are_ _____ many high mountains in Asia.

1. _____ several cars in the accident.
2. _____ no people in the cars now.
3. _____ two policemen near the accident.
4. _____ one ambulance at the scene of the accident.
5. _____ many people on the sidewalk.
6. _____ one reporter from the newspaper.

7. _____ no injuries to the people.

8. _____ three nervous passengers close to the cars.

9. _____ one driver by the police car.

10. _____ an accident here almost every day.

EXERCISE 2 Use *There isn't / There aren't* to complete the following sentences.

Example: _There aren't_ any trees on the moon.

1. _____ a lion at that zoo.

2. _____ any soda machines near the arcade.

3. _____ many children at the playground.

4. _____ a child on the swings.

5. _____ a monkey in the Monkey House.

6. _____ a gorilla outside his cave.

7. _____ any tigers in their pens.

8. _____ any cars in the parking lot.

9. _____ many birds in the trees.

10. _____ any hot dogs on the grill.

EXERCISE 3 Use the words given to make a statement about your school, using *There + be*.

Example: auditorium / at my school   _There isn't an auditorium at my school._

computers / at my school   _There are many computers at my school._

1. chalkboards / in the classrooms _____

2. drinking fountains / in the hallways _____

3. computer(s) / in my classroom _____

4. gym / in the building _____

5. television(s) / in the lounge _____

6. pictures / on the walls _____

7. library / in the building _____

8. books / in the library _____

9. children / at the school _____

10. animals / in the classrooms _____

11. desk(s) / in the office(s) _____

12. typewriter / in the main office _____

PRACTICE 18 Questions with *There*

IS / ARE + THERE	NOUN PHRASE	PREPOSITIONAL PHRASE	SHORT ANSWER
Is there	a laundry room	in your building?	No, there isn't.
Are there	(any) cabinets	in the kitchen?	Yes, there are.

HOW MANY + NOUN PHRASE	ARE + THERE	PREPOSITIONAL PHRASE	SHORT ANSWER
How many closets	***are there***	in your apartment?	There are three.
How many apartments	***are there***	in your building?	There are ten.

LANGUAGE NOTES:

1. We usually use *any* to introduce a plural noun in a *yes / no* question:
   Are there any empty apartments in your building?
2. Do not make a contraction for a short *yes* answer:
   Is there an elevator in your building?   Yes, there *is*.   [**Not:** Yes, there's.]

EXERCISE 1 Read the following questions with *there*. Then write a short answer.

Example: Are there mountains in Switzerland?   (yes)   *Yes, there are.* _____

1. Are there beaches in Hawaii?   (yes)

   _____

2. Is there a lot of snow in the Philippines?   (no)

   _____

3. Are there deserts in Egypt?   (yes)

   _____

4. Are there tall buildings in New York City?   (yes)

   _____

5. Are there deserts in Japan?   (no)

   _____

6. Is there a rain forest in South America?   (yes)

   _____

7. Are there cathedrals in Paris?   (yes)

   _____

8. Is there a king of the United States?   (no)

   _____

EXERCISE 2 Circle the correctly worded questions below.

Example: (Is there a telephone?) / Are there a telephone?

1. Are there a bank nearby our job? / Is there a bank nearby our job?
2. Are there any police in the stadium? / Is there any police in the stadium?
3. Are there any people around here? / Is there any people around here?
4. Is there a library in this school? / Are there a library in this school?
5. Is there many stores on your street? / Are there many stores on your street?

EXERCISE 3 Unscramble the words below to form questions. Then choose the correct answer from the box and write a short answer.

seven	twelve	fifty	seven	nine	seven	five	~~sixty~~	thirty-one

Example: seconds / how many / there / are / in a minute

How many seconds are there in a minute?   *There are sixty.*

1. states / how many / the United States / are / there / in

   _____   _____

2. there / how many / in a rainbow / colors / are

   _____   _____

3. in a year / how many / months / are / there

   _____   _____

4. are / there / how many / in December / days

   _____   _____

5. in our solar system / there / how many / planets / are

   _____   _____

6. how many / there / are / in a week / days

   _____   _____

7. on the Earth / how many / are / continents / there

   _____   _____

8. how many / are / fingers / there / on one hand

   _____   _____

PRACTICE 19 Articles and Quantity Words

SINGULAR INDEFINITE	DEFINITE	EXPLANATION
I live in **a** big building. There's **a** janitor in the building.	**The** building is near the college. **The** janitor lives on the first floor.	We introduce a singular noun with the indefinite articles (*a* or *an*). When we refer to this noun again, we use the definite article *the*.
	May I speak to **the** landlord? He lives on **the** third floor.	We use *the* before a singular noun if this noun is the only one or if the speaker and listener share an experience and are referring to the same one.

PLURAL INDEFINITE	DEFINITE	EXPLANATION
My basement has **(some)** washing machines. Are there **(any)** dryers?	**The** washing machines are in the basement. Where are **the** dryers?	We introduce a plural noun with *some*, *any*, or no article. When we refer to this noun again, we use the definite article *the*.
	The washing machines don't work.	We use *the* before a plural noun if the speaker and the listener share the same experience.

LANGUAGE NOTES:
1. We don't use an article when we refer to something *in general*:
   Washing machines save time. Computer games are fun.
2. We use *any* with questions and negative statements.
3. We use *some* with positive statements.

EXERCISE 1 Circle the correct word from the choices given.

Example: Do you have a / the pencil?

Conversation 1

A: Is there (1) a / the computer in the office?

B: Yes, there are two computers. There is a laptop and a desktop.

A: I want to use (2) a / the desktop computer.

Conversation 2

A: I need a cup.

B: There are (3) <u>some / any</u> cups in (4) <u>a / the</u> kitchen. Which cup do you want?
There's a red one and (5) <u>a / the</u> green one.

A: I want (6) <u>a / the</u> green cup.

Conversation 3

A: Is there (7) <u>a / the</u> grocery store in our neighborhood?

B: Yes, there is. What do you need?

A: I need to buy (8) <u>any / some</u> apples.

B: Where is (9) <u>a / the</u> store, exactly?

A: It's on Maple Street, on (10) <u>a / the</u> left side of (11) <u>a / the</u> street.

B: Thanks for (12) <u>a / the</u> information.

EXERCISE 2 These are conversations between neighbors. Fill in each blank with *the, a, an, some,* or *any*.

Conversation 1

A: Is there (1) _____ *a* _____ video store in our neighborhood?

B: Yes, there are several video stores in (2) _____ neighborhood.

A: Are (3) _____ videos cheap?

B: Yes, it costs only (4) _____ dollar for each video.

Conversation 2

A: Is there (5) _____ gym in this building?

B: Yes, there is.

A: Where's (6) _____ gym?

B: It's in (7) _____ basement.

A: Are there (8) _____ exercise machines in

(9) _____ gym?

B: Yes, there are.

A: I want to lift weights.

B: (10) _____ weight machines are really hard to use.

Conversation 3

A: Are there (11) _____ school supply stores around here?

B: No, but there is (12) _____ office supply store.

A: Great! Where is (13) _____ office supply store?

B: It's in the Empire Building, on (14) _____ first floor.

PRACTICE 20 Frequency Words with the Simple Present Tense, and the Position of Frequency Words

FREQUENCY WORD	FREQUENCY	EXAMPLE
always	100 percent	Mother's Day is **always** in May.
usually		I **usually** take my mother out to dinner.
often		People **often** wear green on St. Patrick's Day.
sometimes		I **sometimes** watch the parade.
rarely / seldom		We **rarely** give flowers to children.
never	0 percent	Businesses are **never** closed for Valentine's Day.

SUBJECT	FREQUENCY WORD	VERB	COMPLEMENT
I	**usually**	buy	a card for my mother.
People	**never**	take	the day off for St. Patrick's Day.

SUBJECT	*BE*	FREQUENCY WORD	COMPLEMENT
Businesses	are	**never**	closed for St. Patrick's Day.
Mother's Day	is	**always**	in May.

EXERCISE 1 Change the percentage into a frequency word in the sentences below. More than one answer may be possible.

Example: (100 percent) Taro _____ *always* _____ wears a hat.

1. (100 percent) Selina and Rick _____ go to the beach on summer weekends.

2. (0 percent) They _____ stay home.

3. (40 percent) _____ they bring their dog.

4. (80 percent) They _____ drive to the beach.

5. (20 percent) They _____ take the train.

6. (60 percent) They _____ bring friends with them.

7. (20 percent) They _____ go swimming. They like to sit in the sun.

8. (100 percent) Harold and Jane _____ stay in the city.

9. (80 percent) They _____ eat dinner at home.

10. (20 percent) They _____ eat dinner at restaurants.

11. (0 percent) They _____ eat at very expensive restaurants.

12. (40 percent) _____ Jane looks for bargains at the grocery store.

Unscramble the words below to form statements.

Example: does / always / my mother / the shopping grocery

My mother always does the grocery shopping.

1. cooks / always / dinner / my father _____

2. my mother / the dishes / usually / does _____

3. the dishes / sometimes / do / I _____

4. does / my brother / seldom / anything _____

5. we / watch / often / TV / after dinner _____

Add an appropriate verb to complete each statement.

Example: Sometimes / I / on weekends.

Sometimes I make cookies on weekends.

1. I / always / after school. _____

2. I / never / on weekdays. _____

3. I / usually / on Saturday. _____

4. I / rarely / on weeknights. _____

5. I / often / on weekends. _____

6. Sometimes / I / in the morning. _____

Add a frequency word to each sentence to make a true statement about yourself.

Example: I listen to rock music.

I rarely listen to rock music.

1. I clean the house. _____

2. I am late to class. _____

3. I watch television. _____

4. I take the bus. _____

5. I take notes in class. _____

6. I am tired during the day. _____

7. I write letters. _____

8. I write e-mails. _____

PRACTICE 21 *Yes / No Questions with Ever*

DO / DOES	SUBJECT	EVER	MAIN VERB	COMPLEMENT	SHORT ANSWER
Do	you	*ever*	celebrate	Mother's Day?	Yes, I always do.
Does	your father	*ever*	cook	the meals?	No, he never does.

BE	SUBJECT	EVER		COMPLEMENT	SHORT ANSWER
Is	Mother's Day	*ever*		on a Sunday?	Yes, it always is.
Are	you	*ever*		bored in class?	No, I never am.

LANGUAGE NOTES:

1. We use *ever* in a *yes / no* question when we want an answer that has a frequency word.
2. In a short answer, the frequency word comes between the subject and the verb.

EXERCISE 1 Rewrite each question with *ever* in the correct position.

Example: Do you celebrate your birthday?

Do you ever celebrate your birthday?

1. Do you walk to school? _____
2. Are you homesick? _____
3. Is your best friend busy? _____
4. Does your family enjoy the beach? _____
5. Do you think about the environment? _____
6. Is school vacation in the spring? _____
7. Are children in school on Sunday? _____
8. Are people polite in public? _____
9. Do you eat dinner alone? _____
10. Are you interested in movies? _____

EXERCISE 2 Write short answers to the questions above. Use frequency words in your answers.

Example: Do you ever celebrate your birthday? _Yes, I usually do._

1. _____   3. _____
2. _____   4. _____

5. _____   8. _____
6. _____   9. _____
7. _____   10. _____

EXERCISE 3 Write short answers to the questions below. Use frequency words in your answers.

Example: Do you ever walk to school?   *No, I never do.* _____

1. Do you ever eat pizza for breakfast?   _____
2. Are you ever sleepy in the morning?   _____
3. Is it ever cold in the springtime?   _____
4. Do you ever read the newspaper?   _____
5. Does your teacher ever speak your language?   _____
6. Do the students in your class ever use English in class?   _____
7. Are you ever busy on weekends?   _____
8. Is your English class ever held in the summer?   _____

EXERCISE 4 Write questions using the verbs and complements below. Then write answers. In each answer, include some more information.

Example: do homework after school

Do you ever do homework after school? _____

Yes, I usually do homework after school at the library. _____

1. ever speak English outside of class

_____

_____

2. ever read English books

_____

_____

3. ever dream in English

_____

_____

4. ever surf the Internet

_____

_____

5. ever watch television

_____

_____

Practice 21   45

PRACTICE 22 Frequency Expressions and Questions with *How Often*

HOW OFTEN	DO / DOES	SUBJECT	VERB	COMPLEMENT	ANSWER
How often	*do*	you	visit	your mother?	Once a week.
How often	*does*	the mail	come?		Every day.

LANGUAGE NOTES:

1. Expressions that show frequency include: *every day (week, month, year), every other day (week, month, year), from time to time, once in a while, once a day (week, month, year), twice a day (week, month, year),* and *a few times a day (week, month, year).*
2. Frequency expressions can come at the beginning or at the end of a sentence.

EXERCISE 1 Put the words for each statement in correct order. Add a question mark (?). Then write a short answer.

Example: novels / often / do / how / you / read

How often do you read novels?   Answer: *Once in a while.*

1. go / how / do / to restaurants / often / you

   _____   Answer: _____

2. how / you / often / see / do / your friends

   _____   Answer: _____

3. English homework / do / how / you / do / often

   _____   Answer: _____

4. how / often / go grocery shopping / do / you

   _____   Answer: _____

5. often / do / how / TV / you / watch

   _____   Answer: _____

6. do / you / use / often / how / your dictionary

   _____   Answer: _____

7. write / often / do / you / how / letters

   _____   Answer: _____

8. do / often / you / go / how / to the movies

   _____   Answer: _____

Ramon's Schedule

- Play basketball, Wednesday
- Do grammar homework, Mondays and Wednesdays
- Work out at the gym, Mondays, Wednesdays, and Fridays
- Update vocabulary cards, Monday to Friday
- Write composition, Thursday
- Bring grammar book to school, Monday to Thursday
- Practice English conversation with Angela, first Saturday of every month
- Read chapter in reading book, the first and third Tuesdays of every month
- Do listening homework, Sunday to Saturday
- Relax and have fun! Sundays

EXERCISE 2 Write **questions** for the answers given below using *How often.*

Example: *How often does he go to drawing class?*
He goes to drawing class once a week.

1. _____
He plays basketball once a week.

2. _____
He works out at the gym a few times a week.

3. _____
He does his listening homework every day.

4. _____
He practices English with Angela once a month.

EXERCISE 3 Write answers about Ramon's activities using expressions that show frequency.

Example: How often does he go to drawing class?
He goes to drawing class once a week.

1. How often does he do grammar homework?

   _____

2. How often does he update vocabulary cards?

   _____

3. How often does he bring a grammar book to school?

   _____

4. How often does he relax and have fun?

   _____

Practice 22   **47**

PRACTICE 23 Prepositions of Time

PREPOSITION	EXAMPLE

On: days and dates	When do you do laundry?
	  On Saturdays.
	When do Canadian people celebrate New Year's Eve?
	  On December 31.

In: months	When do British people celebrate Christmas? *In* December.
In: years	When do Americans vote for a president? *In* 2000, 2004, 2008, and so on.
At: specific time of day	What time does the class start? *At* eight o'clock.
In the morning	When do you work? *In* the morning.
In the afternoon *In* the evening	When do you go to school? *In* the evening.
At night	When do you call your family? *At* night.
In: seasons	When do we have a vacation? *In* the summer.
From . . . to: a beginning and ending time	What hours do they work? *From* nine to five.

EXERCISE 1 Circle the correct preposition to complete the sentence.

Example: I will graduate from college (in) / on 2004.

1. People often go to church <u>at / on</u> Sunday.
2. My husband works <u>from / for</u> nine to six.
3. <u>On / In</u> the winter we read a lot of books.
4. I put the cat outside <u>on / at</u> night.
5. My mother's birthday is <u>for / in</u> April.
6. I want to buy a car <u>in / at</u> 2005.
7. <u>At / In</u> the morning, we walk for exercise.
8. The movie is <u>from / at</u> 7:30 to 9:30.
9. I go to bed <u>at / from</u> midnight.
10. My wedding anniversary is <u>in / on</u> August 17.
11. He likes to relax <u>on / in</u> the evening.
12. She enjoys long walks <u>in / at</u> the fall.

EXERCISE 2 Fill in the blanks with the correct prepositions.

Example: I usually go to bed late _____ *at* _____ night.

I usually wake up (1) _____ 6:30 on school days. I take a shower,

and (2) _____ around 6:50 I eat breakfast. I always feel sleepy

(3) _____ the morning. I catch my train (4) _____

7:36. (5) _____ Mondays, the train is very crowded.

(6) _____ Fridays, I sometimes get a seat. I study English

(7) _____ the train. I have two classes (8) _____

the morning and one (9) _____ the afternoon. I go to school

(10) _____ 9:00 (11) _____ 3:30. I am at my job

(12) _____ 4:30 (13) _____ 6:30. I work at an ice

cream shop, so I like my job (14) _____ the summer, but I hate my job

(15) _____ the winter. It's too cold!

EXERCISE 3 Answer these questions using prepositions of time. Use a long or short answer.

Example: When do you usually go to bed?
    I usually go to bed at 11:30.   **or** *At 11:30.*

1. When do you usually wake up? _____
2. What time do you eat breakfast? _____
3. What time do you leave for school? _____
4. What time does school start? _____
5. What time do you get home? _____
6. What time do you eat dinner? _____
7. When do you wake up on weekends? _____
8. When do you do your homework? _____
9. When do you talk on the telephone? _____
10. When do you use a computer? _____
11. When do you watch TV? _____
12. When is your birthday? _____
13. When is the most important holiday in your country? _____
14. When do you relax? _____
15. When is it cold in your country? _____

PRACTICE 24 Possessive Forms of Nouns

NOUN	ENDING	EXAMPLE
Singular noun: father mother	Add apostrophe + s.	I use my **father's** last name. I don't use my **mother's** last name.
Plural noun ending in s: parents boys	Add apostrophe only.	My **parents'** names are Ethel and Herman. Ted and Mike are **boys'** names.
Irregular plural noun: children women	Add apostrophe + s.	What are your **children's** names? Marilyn and Sandra are **women's** names.
Names that end in s: Mr. Harris Charles	Add apostrophe only. **or** Add apostrophe + s	Do you know **Mr. Harris'** wife? **or** Do you know **Charles's** wife?

LANGUAGE NOTE:

We use the possessive form for people and other living things. For inanimate
objects, we usually use the form *the* _____ *of*

_____ .

Washington College is the name of my school.

EXERCISE 1 Some of the following sentences can show possession with apostrophes (*'s* or *'*).
Rewrite these sentences. Write "no change" for the others.

Example: The hat of my father is new.   *My father's hat is new.* _____

The color of the house is white. *no change* _____

1. I always eat the dinners of my mother. _____

2. The name of this book is *More Grammar Practice*. _____

3. The name of my cat is Nemo. _____

4. What are the names of your best friends? _____

5. Who is the husband of Phyllis? _____

6. The roof of the house is white. _____

7. I like to go to the house of my friend. _____

8. New Language Center is the name of my school. _____

9. The toy of the baby is on the floor. _____

10. Where is the food of the children? _____

11. Red and blue are the favorite colors of my brother. _____

12. The color of the car is green. _____

13. This is the pen of my teacher. _____

14. The job of the doctor is to help sick people. _____

15. Do you live in the house of your parents? _____

16. The subject of this class is English. _____

17. The name of the mother of my best friend is Mabel. _____

18. The glass of the window is clear. _____

EXERCISE 2 Write 10 sentences using words from the box below. Use the possessive form of the noun when possible. You can use other words too.

Example: *My mother's favorite color is yellow.*

my mother	car
my father	pen
my best friend	book
my sister/brother	clothes
my teacher	favorite color
my hometown	shoes
Andre	pet
Lee	name
Carlos	job
Jenna	game

1. _____

2. _____

3. _____

4. _____

5. _____

6. _____

7. _____

8. _____

9. _____

10. _____

PRACTICE 25 Possessive Adjectives

SUBJECT PRONOUN	POSSESSIVE ADJECTIVE	EXAMPLE
I	my	I like **my** name.
you	your	You're a new student. What's **your** name?
he	his	He likes **his** name.
she	her	She doesn't like **her** name.
it	its	Is this your dog? Is it friendly? What's **its** name?
we	our	We use **our** nicknames.
they	their	They are new friends. **Their** last name is Jackson.

LANGUAGE NOTE:

Be careful not to confuse *his* and *her:*

My mother lives in Chicago. *Her* brother lives in Las Vegas.

EXERCISE 1 Fill in the blanks with the correct subject, pronoun, or possessive adjective from the choices enclosed in parentheses.

Example: (his / he) In the morning, _____*he*_____ washes _____*his*_____ face.

1. (my / I) _____ mother and _____ go shopping this week.
2. (they / their) _____ family visits when _____ have a vacation.
3. (our / we) _____ love _____ new apartment.
4. (her / she) _____ buys a tree for _____ garden.
5. (it / its) _____ looks great in _____ new place by the roses.
6. (your / you) _____ and _____ brother look just the same!
7. (he / his) _____ buys _____ jackets at an expensive store.
8. (I / my) _____ teacher and _____ solve many math problems.
9. (their / they) _____ grades aren't so good. _____ usually do better.
10. (we / our) _____ want to read _____ books tonight.
11. (its / it) _____ paw is hurt and _____ needs medical attention.
12. (she / her) _____ rides the bus to _____ job on weekdays.
13. (you / your) _____ dinner is ready. Are _____ ready to eat?
14. (his / he) _____ watches _____ favorite show on Fridays.
15. (my / I) _____ always lose _____ pearl earrings.
16. (they / their) _____ and _____ parents cook wonderful meals.

EXERCISE 2 Fill in the blanks with the possessive adjectives that refer to the subject.

Example: I like _____*my*_____ teacher.

1. He opens _____ book.

2. She loves _____ grandfather.

3. The cat likes _____ toy.

4. Many teachers give _____ students too much homework.

5. Sometimes my sister does _____ homework in the bathtub.

6. Mr. Johnson buys _____ shoes in the spring.

7. Do you use _____ dictionary every day?

8. I bring _____ daughter to work with me sometimes.

9. We wear _____ coats in winter.

10. Ms. Winfrey always tells _____ children to eat
    _____ dinner.

11. Some people wash _____ cars every day.

12. He uses _____ cell phone in class.

13. She keeps _____ pencils in _____ bag.

14. The mouse eats _____ cheese.

15. Most people love _____ parents.

16. Sometimes Lisa eats _____ lunch in the morning.

17. I carry _____ bag everywhere.

18. We need _____ books now.

19. She eats _____ lunch at the same time every day.

20. Two of my friends do _____ homework together.

21. He talks to _____ grandmother every week on the phone.

22. The computer needs _____ hard drive.

23. You often clean _____ car.

24. You always buy _____ shoes at the department store.

25. We usually call _____ mothers on Sunday.

26. Does he want _____ test grade now?

27. This bag always breaks at _____ strap.

28. I am hungry for _____ lunch right now.

EXAMPLE	EXPLANATION
You don't know my name. I know **yours.**	*yours = your name*
Your name is easy for Americans. **Mine** is hard.	*mine = my name*

LANGUAGE NOTE:

1. When we use a possessive pronoun, we omit the noun.
   Her children have English names. *Hers* have English names.
   My children have Spanish names. *Mine* have Spanish names.

SUBJECT PRONOUN	POSSESSIVE ADJECTIVE	POSSESSIVE PRONOUN
I	my	mine
you	your	yours
he	his	his
she	her	hers
it	its	—
we	our	ours
they	their	theirs
who	whose	whose

EXERCISE 1 Rewrite the second sentence of each item below, replacing the underlined words with a possessive pronoun.

Example: Your coat is brown. My coat is blue.
Your coat is brown. Mine is blue.

1. My birthday is in January. Your birthday is in March.

   _____

2. His cat is white. Her cat is black.

   _____

3. I like my brother. Do you like your brother?

   _____

4. My teacher is strict. Is your teacher strict?

   _____

5. Can I use your pen? My pen doesn't work.

   _____

6. Whose socks are these? Whose socks are those?

   _____

7. My mother comes from Sri Lanka. <u>Ravi's mother</u> comes from India.

   _____

8. Yoko's dress is red. <u>Julie's dress</u> is red too.

   _____

9. Miguel's house is big. <u>Peter's house</u> is small.

   _____

10. Antonio and Carlotta's jobs are difficult. <u>Nina and Matt's jobs</u> are easy.

    _____

11. You have an old red car. <u>Our car</u> is new.

    _____

12. My hair is red. <u>Their hair</u> is red too.

    _____

13. Your shirts are pink. <u>My shirts</u> are green.

    _____

14. Their class is boring. <u>Our class</u> is interesting.

    _____

15. My parents always watch TV. Do <u>your parents</u> always watch TV?

    _____

EXERCISE 2 Joanna is comparing herself to her classmates. Complete Joanna's second sentence.

Example: My hair is long. (he / short) *His is short.* _____

1. My glasses are made of silver wire. (she / brown plastic)

   _____

2. My pet is a Siamese cat. (he / old parrot)

   _____

3. My job is in the city. (they / in the country)

   _____

4. My apartment has two bedrooms. (you / one bedroom)

   _____

5. My parents are careful with money. (their / spend a lot of money)

   _____

PRACTICE 27 The Subject and the Object

EXAMPLE	EXPLANATION
S V O Bob likes Mary. We like movies.	The subject (S) comes before the verb (V). The object (O) comes after the verb. The object is a person or a thing.
S V O S V O Bob likes Mary because she helps him. S V O S V O I like movies because they entertain me.	We can use pronouns for the subject and the object.

LANGUAGE NOTE:

There can be more than one subject, verb, or object in a sentence:

  S   S
Dogs and cats are favorite pets.

      V   V
She walks and jogs for exercise.

          O   O   O
I need soap, toothpaste, and a hairbrush.

EXERCISE 1 Write S, V, or O over the subjects, verbs, and objects of these sentences.

                  S   V   O
Example: She smells the roses.

1. I eat bananas.

2. Michael knows Dorothy.

3. He is a doctor.

4. They have money.

5. She makes hats.

6. Maggie and Tim grow vegetables.

7. It isn't a cloud.

8. We love English.

EXERCISE 2 Fill in the blanks with a subject to complete these sentences. Use the names of students in your class as the subjects of the sentences.

Example: _Chen_____ wears nice clothes.

1. _____ speaks English well.

2. _____ has a car.

3. _____ likes classical music.

4. _____ reads many books.

5. _____ is never late to class.

6. _____ takes good notes.

7. _____ has a job.

8. _____ helps me study.

9. _____ has a nice smile.

10. _____ does homework.

EXERCISE 3 Fill in the blanks with an object to complete these sentences. Use your own ideas.

Example: I need *a new notebook* _____ .

1. I have _____ .
2. I want _____ .
3. She loves _____ .
4. I am _____ .
5. I like _____ .

6. He studies _____ .
7. My teacher likes _____ .
8. My friend is _____ .
9. My friend wears _____ .
10. Everyone likes _____ .

EXERCISE 4 Write S, V, or O over the subjects, verbs, and objects in this paragraph.

Example: The fog covers the city.
         S   V   O

Weather affects everyone. Some people love bad weather, and some people hate bad weather. In the city, businessmen and businesswomen use umbrellas in the rain. The umbrellas keep them from getting wet. In the city, people dislike the rain. People on vacation don't like rain. Rain keeps people inside. People play sports outside on vacation, and rain stops outdoor baseball games and basketball games.

Even so, some people like the rain. Farmers like rain because it helps the crops. Sun, rain, and good earth make the plants grow. Rain helps the crops become food. Sometimes the rain stops and the vegetables don't grow. Then supermarkets charge more money for vegetables. Luckily, farmers have irrigation systems. Irrigation systems water the plants and vegetables. People dislike bad weather, but good weather and bad weather grow our food.

The Subject and the Object

PRACTICE 28 Object Pronouns

SUBJECT	OBJECT PRONOUN	EXAMPLE SUBJECT	VERB	OBJECT PRONOUN
I	me	You	love	me.
you	you	I	love	you.
he	him	She	loves	him.
she	her	He	loves	her.
it	it	We	love	it.
we	us	They	love	us.
they	them	We	love	them.

LANGUAGE NOTES:

1. We can use an object pronoun to substitute for an object noun:
   I love *my mother*. I visit *her* once a week.
2. We use *them* for plural people and things:
   I have two brothers. You know *them*.
3. An object pronoun can follow a preposition:
   My sister has a son. She always talks about *him*.

EXERCISE 1 Fill in each blank with the object pronoun of the underlined word.

Example: I eat ice cream. I eat *it* _____.

1. I see <u>stars</u> at night.   I see _____.

2. You help <u>your brother</u>.   You help _____.

3. He cleans <u>the garage</u>.   He cleans _____.

4. We like <u>chicken</u> very much.   We like _____ very much.

5. They need <u>a two-bedroom apartment</u>.   They need _____.

6. I open <u>boxes</u> at work.   I open _____ at work.

7. She writes <u>a composition</u>.   She writes _____.

8. It hits <u>the car</u> suddenly.   It hits _____ suddenly.

9. The trees drop <u>their leaves</u> in fall.   The trees drop _____ in fall.

10. He loves <u>his wife</u> very much.   He loves _____ very much.

11. My mother often calls <u>you</u>.   My mother often calls _____.

12. Every year he promises <u>Julia and me</u>.   Every year he promises _____.

EXERCISE 2 Fill in the blanks with the object pronoun of the underlined word.

Example: I understand you, and you understand ____me____.

1. Romeo loves Juliet, and she loves _____ too.
2. I take care of my parents, and my parents take care of _____.
3. Her name is Elizabeth, but we call _____ Beth.
4. I like sushi. Do you like _____ too?
5. I speak English in class, but I don't speak _____ at home.
6. John walks toward George and looks at _____.
7. These are our photo albums. Please look at _____.
8. When we are late, out boss gets angry at _____.
9. My friends sometimes write to me, and I sometimes write to _____.
10. I talk to her, and she talks to _____.
11. We help them, and they help _____.
12. This is a new outfit. Do you like _____?
13. These are new shoes. Do you like _____?
14. She is our English teacher. We like _____ a lot.
15. Francisco is my best friend. I like being with _____.
16. This is a great CD. Do you like _____?

EXERCISE 3 Two friends are talking on the phone. Fill in the blanks with appropriate object pronouns.

Example: How often do you write to ____them____?

A: I like Miami, but I miss my parents.
B: How often do you see (1) _____?
A: About twice a year. They often call (2) _____, and sometimes I send (3) _____ e-mail.
B: How about your sister Joanne? Do you talk with (4) _____ much?
A: Not much. I miss (5) _____ a lot.
B: Does she come visit (6) _____?
A: No. She wants to, but hotels are too expensive, and my apartment is too small.

PRACTICE 29 Questions about the Subject or about the Complement

Compare the following statements and related questions about the complement and about the subject.

WH- WORD	DO / DOES	SUBJECT	VERB	COMPLEMENT
		Susan	needs	something.
What	does	she	need?	
		She	needs	a new TV.
		My parents	live	in Peru.
Where	do	your parents	live?	
		They	live	in Colombia.
		Your sister	likes	someone.
Who(m)	does	she	like?	
		She	likes	her boyfriend.

SUBJECT	VERB	COMPLEMENT	SHORT ANSWER
Someone	has	my book.	
Who	has	my book?	Tom does.
Someone	needs	help.	
Who	needs	help?	I do.

LANGUAGE NOTES:

1. Most *wh–* questions in the present tense use *do* or *does*. These questions ask about the complement:

   He lives *in Peru.*   I see *someone.*

   Where does he live?   *Who(m)* do you see?

2. Some *wh–* questions ask about the subject:

   Someone needs help.   *Something* is wrong.

   Who needs help?   *What* is wrong?

EXERCISE 1 Choose the correct word to fill in the blanks.

Example: (who / what) *What* _____ is your name?

1. (who / what) _____ do you do for work?

2. (where / what) _____ does he go after class?

3. (whom / who) _____ is your teacher?

4. (what / who) _____ is your phone number?

5. (where / who) _____ do you keep your bicycle?

6. (who / whom) _____ do you like? (formal wording)

7. (who / whom) _____ do you trust the most? (informal wording)

8. (what / where) _____ do you study after class?

9. (who / whom) _____ cuts your hair?

10. (who / what) _____ does she need for school supplies?

11. (whom / who) _____ does he talk to? (informal wording)

12. (what / who) _____ is the temperature today?

EXERCISE 2 Make questions from the following words. Add a question mark.

Example: Spanish / speaks / who   *Who speaks Spanish?* _____

1. does / Anna / where / walk   _____

2. eat / what / my teacher /does   _____

3. what / Paolo / does / sing   _____

4. what / I / every day / do / carry   _____

5. studies / in my class / who / hard   _____

6. like / does / my father / what   _____

7. feels / uncomfortable / what   _____

8. visits / who / me   _____

EXERCISE 3 Make a question about the complement in each of the following statements. Change the pronouns as necessary.

Example: *Where does your best friend live?* _____

My best friend lives in Peru.

1. _____ Tom likes apples.

2. _____ I have a new car.

3. _____ Karen likes Bob.

4. _____ She sees a rose.

5. _____ They write poems.

6. _____ He drives a truck.

7. _____ Juan makes toys.

8. _____ My parents write to them.

9. _____ My brother always eats hamburgers.

10. _____ Julie thinks tennis is great.

Practice 29   61

PRACTICE **30** Forms and Uses of the Present Continuous Tense

SUBJECT	BE	VERB + –ING
I	am	reading.
You	are	learning.
We	are	studying.
They	are	practicing.
Jim and Sue	are	writing.
He	is	eating.
She	is	sitting.
It	is	sleeping.
Jim	is	standing.

LANGUAGE NOTES:

1. We can make a contraction with the subject pronoun and a form of *be*.
   Most nouns can also make a contraction with *is*:
   Dan's writing a letter.   We're studying verbs.
2. To form the negative, put *not* after the verb *am / is / are*:
   Dan *isn't* writing a composition.   I'm *not* sleeping in class.
3. When the subject is doing two or more things, we don't repeat the verb
   be after *and*:
   Children are making a snowman and throwing snowballs.

EXAMPLES	USE
Dan *is writing* a letter to his family now. It's *snowing* now.	To show that an action is in progress at this moment.
Dan and his roommate *are gaining* weight. Dan *is writing* a term paper this semester.	To show a long-term action that is in progress. It may not be happening at this exact moment.
He *is wearing* a sweater. He *is sitting* near the window.	To describe a state or condition, using verbs such as *sit, stand, wear,* or *sleep*.

EXERCISE 1   Fill in the missing part of each sentence.

Example: He's eat*ing*_____ a sandwich.

They _____*are*_____ playing baseball.

1. I'm think _____ of you.

2. My mother and father _____ riding the train.

3. Karla _____ wearing a new dress.

4. The students in my class are speak _____ English.

5. He's learn _____ Chinese.

6. My teacher _____ writing on the board.

7. I _____ taking notes.

8. The boats _____ sailing on the water.

9. The sun _____ shining down.

10. My brother is study _____ computer science.

EXERCISE 2 Write a sentence in the present continuous tense using the words given.

Example: the cat / sleep   *The cat is sleeping.* _____

1. my brother / cook / dinner   _____

2. my sister / talk / on the telephone   _____

3. my father / use / his computer   _____

4. my mother / exercise   _____

5. the dog / eat   _____

6. I / do my homework   _____

7. the earth / turn   _____

8. the sun / set   _____

9. plants / grow   _____

10. I / think / about my friend   _____

EXERCISE 3 Answer these questions using the present continuous tense with true information about yourself.

Example: Who is helping you with your homework?
   My friend Lee is helping me with my homework. _____

1. What are you doing now?   _____

2. What are you thinking about?   _____

3. Where are you sitting?   _____

4. What are you writing with?   _____

5. Is anyone sitting near you?   _____

6. Who is teaching you English (this semester)?   _____

7. What other classes are you taking?   _____

8. What are you wearing?   _____

9. Are you sleeping?   _____

10. Are you eating?   _____

PRACTICE 31 Spelling of the *–ing* Form

RULE	VERB	*–ING* FORM
Add *–ing* to most verbs. (*Note:* Do not drop the *y* from the base form.)	eat go study	eat*ing* go*ing* study*ing*
For a one-syllable verb that ends in a consonant + vowel + consonant (CVC), double the final consonant and add *–ing*.	p l a n ↓ ↓ ↓ C V C s t o p ↓ ↓ ↓ C V C s i t ↓ ↓ ↓ C V C	plann*ing* stopp*ing* sitt*ing*
Do not double a final *w, x,* or *y.*	show mix stay	show*ing* mix*ing* stay*ing*
For a two-syllable verb that ends in CVC, double the final consonant only if the last syllable is stressed.	refér admít begín	refer*ring* admit*ting* beginn*ing*
When the last syllable of a two-syllable verb is not stressed, do not double the final consonant.	lísten ópen óffer	listen*ing* open*ing* offer*ing*
If the verb ends in a consonant + *e,* drop the *e* before adding *–ing.*	live take write	liv*ing* tak*ing* writ*ing*

EXERCISE 1 Write the *–ing* form of the verb. Two-syllable verbs that end in CVC have accent marks to show which syllable is stressed.

Example: cook <u>   *cooking*   </u>

1. walk _____
2. talk _____
3. use _____
4. exercise _____

5. eat _____
6. do _____
7. turn _____
8. set _____
9. háppen _____
10. taste _____
11. think _____
12. commít _____
13. drag _____
14. beg _____
15. occúr _____

16. sew _____
17. say _____
18. delay _____
19. defér _____
20. run _____
21. cry _____
22. pay _____
23. grow _____
24. print _____
25. ópen _____

EXERCISE 2 Circle the correct present continuous verb in each sentence.

Example: She deciding / (is deciding) to take the bus.

1. The Jones family are worrying / is worrying about the rent.
2. He are drinking / is drinking hot chocolate.
3. You am reading / read your homework every night this week.
4. Jane is working / working all day.
5. We is having / are having a good time at our job.
6. Those people is waiting / are waiting for the bus.
7. The fish swimming / are swimming up the river.
8. The baseball player is laughing / be laughing at the other team.
9. I are doing / am doing my grammar exercises tonight.
10. It is rain / is raining right now.
11. Our baseball team is winning / are winning today.
12. The hot dog vendor is selling / selling many hot dogs with onions.

EXERCISE 3 Make the following present continuous statements negative.

Example: I am driving to the city tonight.
*I'm not driving to the city tonight.*_____

1. She is sitting beside him. _____
2. He is marrying her soon. _____
3. The flowers are opening in the sunshine. _____
4. I am wiping off the tables. _____
5. The customers are waiting for the check. _____

PRACTICE **32** Questions with the Present Continuous Tense

WH–WORD	BE (+ NOT)	SUBJECT	BE	VERB –ING	COMPLEMENT	SHORT ANSWER
		Dan	**is**	**wearing**	a sweater.	
	Is	Dan		**wearing**	a hat?	No, he **isn't**.
What	**is**	Dan		**wearing?**		
Why	**isn't**	Dan		**wearing**	a hat?	
		Who	**is**	**wearing**	a hat?	
		Children	**are**	**playing**.		
	Are	they		**playing**	inside?	No, they **aren't**.
Where	**are**	they		**playing**	inside?	
Why	**aren't**	they		**playing**	inside?	

LANGUAGE NOTE: When the question is "What . . . doing?" we often
answer with a different verb:

What's he *doing?* He's *writing* a letter.

EXERCISE 1 Fill in the missing parts of the following present-continuous-tense questions.

Example: _Are_ you eating dinner?

1. Is Carol do_____ the dishes?
2. _____ the kids watch _____ TV?
3. What show _____ the kids watch_____?
4. Isn't it snow_____ right now?
5. Who is driv_____ the car?

6. Why _____ you read_____ that book?
7. What video _____ you renting?
8. Where _____ he going?
9. _____ she still sleeping?
10. _____n't you wear_____ socks?

EXERCISE 2 Write a question about each statement using the words given.

Example: A girl is jogging.

   why / jog _Why is she jogging?_

   where / jog _Where is she jogging?_

   why / not / relax _Why isn't she relaxing?_

1. The professor is writing.

   a. what / write _____

66   Practice 32

    b. where / write   _____

    c. why / not / eat   _____

    d. whom / write / to   _____

2. He is leaving.

    a. who / leave   _____

    b. where / he / go   _____

    c. how / he / get / there   _____

    d. what / he / take / with him   _____

3. The leaves are turning brown.

    a. why / leaves / turn brown   _____

    b. which / leaves / turn brown   _____

    c. who / not / water / the plant   _____

4. Jorge is studying English.

    a. why / study / English   _____

    b. where / study / English   _____

    c. who / practice / English / with   _____

    d. why / not / study / computer science   _____

EXERCISE 3 Write a short answer to each question.

Example: Are you dreaming about flying?   (no) *No, I'm not.* _____

1. Is he thinking and worrying about his friends?   (yes) _____

2. Are they going home soon?   (no) _____

3. Is she answering the test questions correctly?   (no) _____

4. Are we studying a useful language?   (yes) _____

5. Is my life changing?   (yes) _____

6. Am I waiting for the wrong train?   (no) _____

7. Is the taxi driver heading in the right direction?   (yes) _____

8. Are you eating lunch at twelve o'clock today?   (no) _____

9. Are they wearing funny shoes?   (yes) _____

10. Am I working and thinking too much?   (yes) _____

EXERCISE 4 What are you doing right now? Write one sentence with two verbs. Use *and*.

_____

Contrast between the Present Continuous and Simple Present Tenses

SIMPLE PRESENT	PRESENT CONTINUOUS
He sometimes **wears** a suit.	He **is wearing** jeans now.
He **doesn't** usually **wear** shorts.	He **isn't wearing** a belt.
Does he ever **wear** a hat?	**Is** he **wearing** a T-shirt?
Yes, he **does.**	No, he **isn't.**
When **does** he **wear** a hat?	What **is** he **wearing?**

EXAMPLE OF USE	EXPLANATION
He **lives** in Brazil. He **goes** to school every day.	Use the simple present tense to talk about a general truth, a habitual activity, or a custom.
Ali **is writing** to his family now.	Use the present continuous tense for an action in progress at this moment.
He **is learning** more and more about American culture all the time.	Use the present continuous tense for a longer action that is in progress at this general time.

LANGUAGE NOTES:

1. When we use *live* in the simple present tense, we mean that this is a person's home. In the present continuous tense, *live* means a temporary or short-term residence:
    He is living in a dorm this semester. His family lives in Jordan.
2. "What do you do (for a living)?" asks about your job. "What are you doing?" asks about your activity at this moment.

EXERCISE 1 Find the mistake in the underlined portion of each of the following sentences; then rewrite the sentence correctly. All statements should be in the present continuous tense.

Example: She is <u>cook</u> in the kitchen now.

She is cooking in the kitchen now.

1. My mother <u>speaking</u> five languages.

    _____

2. They <u>are walk</u> to the movie together.

    _____

3. She <u>doesn't hoping</u> to go to the concert.

    _____

4. I am do my laundry now.

   _____

5. It is snow.

   _____

6. It snowing in the mountains often.

   _____

7. I am not study now because I have a headache.

   _____

8. Listen! She is sing.

   _____

9. What do you doing now?

   _____

10. What is she read?

    _____

11. Do you riding your bicycle every day?

    _____

12. He doesn't working in a hospital.

    _____

EXERCISE 2 Fill in each blank in the conversation with the verb *wear* in either the present simple form (*wear*) or the present continuous form (*wearing*).

Example:

A: Francisco! I almost didn't recognize you. Why aren't you ___*wearing*___ your glasses?

B: I don't (1) _____ my glasses every day. I usually

   (2) _____ them only when I come to class.

A: Well, you are in class now! Shouldn't you be (3) _____ them now?

B: I'm not (4) _____ my glasses because I am

   (5) _____ contact lenses for the first time today.

A: How do you like contact lenses?

B: I don't like them at all. They're very uncomfortable. On the other hand, I like how I look when I

   (6) _____ them.

PRACTICE **34** Future Tense with *Will*

SUBJECT	*WILL*	*(NOT)*	VERB	COMPLEMENT
I	will		buy	a gift.
She	will	not	give	money.
There	will		be	250 people at the wedding.

LANGUAGE NOTES:
1. We use *will* with all persons to form the future tense. *Will* doesn't have an *–s* form.
2. We can make a contraction with the subject pronoun and *will*: *I'll, you'll, he'll, she'll, it'll, we'll,* and *they'll.*
3. Put *not* after *will* to form the negative. The contraction for *will not* is *won't. Will not* is very strong and formal. *Won't* is used often in informal conversation.
4. We can put a frequency word between *will* and the main verb: She will *never* understand American customs.

EXERCISE 1 Unscramble the words to form sentences.

Example: it / today / sunny / be / will   <u>It will be sunny today.</u>

1. doctor / I / become / will / a   _____

2. you / will / in / Germany / live   _____

3. soon / get / will / a new job / he   _____

4. she / will / leave / never   _____

5. will / write / a book / they   _____

6. together / tomorrow / will / play / the girls   _____

7. have / a wonderful time / we / will   _____

8. not / will / rain / it / this weekend   _____

9. a party / will / be / there / not   _____

10. will / never / I / promise / that   _____

EXERCISE 2 Fill in the blanks with appropriate verbs in the future tense. Use *will* or *won't*.

I (1: have) _____ a very busy summer. First, my family

(2: come) _____ to visit me in the city. We (3: go) _____ to

museums and to many nice stores. My brother (4: see) _____ all the big

summer movies. My father and mother (5: not / go) _____ to the movies.

My sister (6: spend) _____ all of her money on shoes. My mother

and father (7: not / spend) _____ money on clothes. They

(8: want) _____ to eat in nice restaurants.

After three days, we (9: travel) _____ to the shore. My family

(10: stay) _____ there for one week. We (11: take) _____ a picnic

lunch to the beach every day. My brother and sister (12: swim) _____ all day. I

(13: play) _____ volleyball with my friends. This (14: be) _____ a

great summer! I hope you (15: come) _____ with us.

EXERCISE 3 Rewrite the sentences below in the future tense with *will*. Some sentences are negative.

Example: He eats a sandwich.   *He will eat a sandwich.*

    She doesn't drink soda.   *She will not drink soda.*

    or *She won't drink soda.*

1. Jessica goes to school.   _____
2. My mother drives her car.   _____
3. Hank needs a hammer.   _____
4. They do not eat cake.   _____
5. Paula walks to work.   _____
6. Arthur studies Spanish.   _____
7. Ken buys a plant.   _____
8. The trees are in bloom.   _____
9. Mina isn't happy.   _____
10. I don't wear glasses.   _____
11. You have good grades.   _____
12. They fly home on holidays.   _____
13. I don't wash the dishes   _____
14. We are happy.   _____
15. My boss has a baby boy.   _____

EXERCISE 4 Imagine how you and the world will be different 20 years from now. Write two complete sentences using *will*.

1. I _____

2. The world _____

PRACTICE 35 Future Tense with *Be Going To*

SUBJECT	BE	(NOT)	GOING TO + VERB	COMPLEMENT
I	am		going to send	a gift.
We	are	not	going to take	a gift to the wedding.
There	are		going to be	musicians at the wedding.
There	is	not	going to be	any rain.

EXERCISE 1 Unscramble the words below to form sentences.

Example: it / going / rain / is / to / this afternoon
It is going to rain this afternoon.

1. going / I / am / to / a teacher / become _____
2. you / study / computers / going / are / to _____
3. to / is / going / quit / he / his job _____
4. the food / isn't / she / to / try / going _____
5. going / are / a baby / to / have / they _____
6. hold / the lawyers / going / are / to / a meeting _____
7. are / to / going / we / to / Mexico / go _____
8. going / a beautiful day / to / be / it / is _____
9. go / you / to / a party / are / going / to _____
10. she / a puppy / buy / is / to / going _____

EXERCISE 2 Rewrite the sentences below using *going to*.

Example: He will eat a sandwich. *He is going to eat a sandwich.*

1. Todd writes a letter. _____
2. My grandmother will walk her dog. _____
3. You need a piece of paper. _____
4. They don't drink water. _____
5. Pam walks to school. _____
6. Andrew is not a salesman. _____
7. We buy apples. _____
8. The TV is making noise. _____

9. Carol is not sad. _____

10. I am doing homework. _____

EXERCISE 3 Write 10 sentences about plans for this weekend using *going to*.

Examples: he / watch TV *He is going to watch TV.* _____

you / not / write a letter *You are not going to write a letter.* _____

1. I / see friends _____

2. you / relax _____

3. she / do grammar homework _____

4. he / not / see a movie _____

5. we / watch a video _____

6. they / not / go to the park _____

7. they / go to the library _____

8. I / listen to music _____

9. it / not / be hot _____

10. you / go to a birthday party _____

EXERCISE 4 What are you going to do this weekend? Write what you *are going to do* and what you *aren't going to do*.

Example: fly a kite *I am not going to fly a kite.* _____

1. write a letter _____

2. go shopping _____

3. work _____

4. study hard _____

5. talk on the phone _____

6. do laundry _____

7. get a haircut _____

8. cook a meal _____

9. sleep _____

10. go to the movies _____

11. play basketball _____

12. take a long walk _____

Practice 35   **73**

Uses of *Will* and *Be Going To*

USE	WILL	BE GOING TO
Prediction	The newlyweds **will** be very happy together.	The newlyweds **are going to** be very happy together.
Fact	Some people **will** give money.	Some people **are going to** give money.
Plan		They **are going to** get married on March 6. I **am going to** buy a gift.
Promise	I **will** always love you.	
Offer to help	**A:** This gift box is heavy. **B:** I'll carry it for you.	

EXERCISE 1 Read the sentences below. On the line provided, write the reason (*prediction, fact, plan, promise,* or *offer to help*) the sentence uses *will* or *be going to.*

Example: I'll do the dishes. _____ *offer to help* _____

1. There will be no cars in the year 2100. _____

2. I'm going to go to the store. _____

3. A band is going to play. _____

4. We're going to have a picnic. _____

5. Next time, I'll do my homework. Really! _____

6. I'll drive you there. _____

7. Maria's going to become a florist. _____

8. I will never do it again. _____

9. The book's going to fall off the table. _____

10. We are going to have a test in this class. _____

11. He'll help you move. He has a truck. _____

12. The world will change in the future. _____

13. It will be cloudy tomorrow. _____

14. You will write the rent check every month. _____

15. I will help you practice your vocabulary. _____

16. I'll take you to the train in the morning. _____

EXERCISE 2 Circle the better expression to complete the sentence.

Example: I am going to /(will) carry it for you.   (offer to help)

1. I will always be / am your friend.   (promise)
2. We will / are going to go grocery shopping tonight.   (plan)
3. He tutors / will tutor the math students next week.   (fact)
4. You will go / go far in your future.   (prediction)
5. She is / will be there at five o'clock.   (fact)
6. I am going to / I'll type that paper for you on my computer.   (offer to help)
7. They are going to / will take a biology class next month.   (plan)
8. I respect / will respect and take care of the environment.   (promise)

EXERCISE 3 Make negative sentences with *be* + *not going to* + the following words.

Example: I / go to the bookstore today

   I'm not going to go to the bookstore today.

1. I / eat dinner with your family this evening   _____
2. He / learn another language   _____
3. You / wash your hair tonight   _____
4. They / travel abroad this year   _____

EXERCISE 4 You will have a picnic with your friends. Write how you think each person will offer to help, using *will*.

Example: Martin lives near a convenience store.

   Martin's offer: *"I'll bring the drinks and plastic cups."*

1. Judy likes cooking.

   Judy's offer: _____
2. Juan has a car.

   Juan's offer: _____
3. Ingrid has a picnic basket.

   Ingrid's offer: _____
4. Tomoko lives near a fruit and vegetable shop.

   Tomoko's offer: _____

WH–WORD	BE (+ *NOT*)	SUBJECT	*BE*	GOING TO +	BASE FORM	COMPLEMENT	SHORT ANSWER
		They	**are**	going to	leave	soon.	
	Are	they		going to	leave	tomorrow?	No, they **aren't**.
When	**are**	they		going to	leave?		
Why	**aren't**	they		going to	leave	tomorrow?	
		Who	**is**	going to	leave?		They **are**.

WH–WORD	WILL / WON'T	SUBJECT	(*WILL*) +	BASE FORM	COMPLEMENT	SHORT ANSWER
		She	**will**	eat	lunch.	
	Will	she		eat	a sandwich?	Yes, she **will**.
What	**will**	she		eat	for lunch?	
Why	**won't**	she		eat	a salad?	
		Who	**will**	eat	lunch?	She **will**.

EXERCISE 1 Unscramble the following words to form questions. Add a question mark.

Example: he / going / another / study / to / language / is

Is he going to study another language?

1. they / to / have / a baby / are / going _____

2. going / we / are / to / married / get _____

3. going / to / take / is / a vacation / who _____

4. she / to / when / graduate / going / is _____

5. so early / why / to eat / dinner / is / he / going _____

6. who / is / to bring / going / the soda _____

7. to quit / your job / you / are / going _____

8. the kitchen / won't / why / clean / you _____

9. will / he / the garbage / take out _____

10. what / bring / will / they / to the party _____

11. why / won't / to / the picnic / you / come _____

12. will / the napkins / buy / who _____

EXERCISE 2 Write a short answer for each question below.

Example: Are you going to watch TV tonight? *No, I'm not.*

1. Is he going to eat dinner at home? *Yes,*
2. Will you do your homework? *Yes,*
3. Are they going to call a friend? *No,*
4. Is she going to write a letter? *Yes,*
5. Are we going to read a new book? *Yes,*
6. Are you going to speak English with the teacher? *Yes,*
7. Will the dog come inside soon? *No,*
8. Are you going to daydream during class? *No,*
9. Is the baby taking a nap? *Yes,*
10. Is she going to sweep the floor? *No,*
11. Will they buy some music CDs? *No,*
12. Will you go to the anniversary party? *Yes,*
13. Will he use your computer? *No,*

EXERCISE 3 Use the terms in the box below to write five questions you have about your own future. Use *will* or *be going to*. Refer to the chart for models.

Example: When / own a business

When will I own a business?

When am I going to own a business?

> make a lot of money / be happy / have a lot of children / be very good at English /
>
> win the lottery / travel abroad / own a home / be famous / have a good job / be healthy

1. When _____
2. When _____
3. When _____
4. When _____
5. When _____

PRACTICE 38 Future Tense + Time / *If* Clause

TIME OR *IF* CLAUSE (SIMPLE PRESENT)	MAIN CLAUSE (FUTURE)
When I **go** to the store,	I **am going to look** at the list of gifts.
If the newlyweds **need** dishes,	I **will buy** dishes for them.

MAIN CLAUSE (FUTURE)	TIME OR *IF* CLAUSE (SIMPLE PRESENT)
I **will go** to the wedding	if I **get** an invitation.
She **is going to thank** the guests	before they **leave.**

LANGUAGE NOTES:

1. The sentences above have two clauses. We use the future tense only in the main clause; we use the simple present tense in the time clause / *if* clause.
2. If the time or *if* clause comes first, we separate the two clauses with a comma.
3. Time clauses suggest a plan for the future.
4. *If* clauses suggest a possibility in the future. The main clause action will not happen if the *if* clause action doesn't come true.

EXERCISE 1 Complete each statement using *will* or *be going to.*

Example: When this class is over, *I will go home.*

   or   *I am going to go home.*

1. Before I finish this exercise, _____
2. When I leave school today, _____
3. When I complete this English class, _____
4. Before I go to sleep tonight, _____
5. _____ when I wake up tomorrow.
6. _____ when I meet my friends.

EXERCISE 2 Complete each statement using *will* or *be going to.*

Example: If I don't eat dinner, *I'm going to feel hungry.*

1. If I don't come to school, _____
2. If I study every day, _____
3. If I don't study every day, _____
4. If I make a lot of money, _____

5. _____ if I don't make a lot of money.

6. _____ if I move to another country.

EXERCISE 3 Fill in the blanks with the correct form of the verb to complete each sentence. Use either *will* or *be going to* for time or *if* clauses.

Example: When I _____*graduate*_____ , I _____*am going to get*_____ a good job.
(graduate)   (get)

1. When I _____ , I _____ a painter.
   (grow up)   (be)

2. If I _____ a lot of wonderful paintings, I _____ famous.
   (paint)   (become)

3. I _____ many of the paintings before I _____ famous.
   (sell)   (become)

4. When people _____ the paintings, I _____ a lot of money.
   (buy)   (make)

5. I _____ a big house when I _____ enough money.
   (buy)   (have)

6. I _____ a party when I _____ into that big house.
   (have)   (move)

7. If I _____ a party, I _____ many movie stars to my
   (have)   (invite)
   house.

8. If I _____ movie stars, there _____ many
   (invite)   (be)
   photographers at the party too.

9. The photographers _____ photos of my paintings when they
   (take)
   _____ them.
   (see)

10. I _____ very famous if I ever _____!
    (become)   (grow up)

EXERCISE 4 Complete the following sentences with *if* or *when* or *before*. (Sometimes two answers are possible.)

1. She is going to buy an enormous mansion _____ she wins $1,000,000.

2. _____ he learns to drive, he is going to take me to work every day.

3. _____ I get home tonight, I am going to make dinner.

4. _____ I get home tonight, I will go to the grocery store.

5. _____ they move to our town, we will be very happy.

PRACTICE 39 Simple Past Tense of Regular Verbs

EXAMPLE	EXPLANATION
The Wright Brothers **dreamed** about flying.	For regular verbs, the simple past tense ends in *–ed*.
They **started** a bicycle business.	
They **invented** the airplane.	

BASE FORM	PAST FORM
dream	dream**ed**
start	start**ed**
invent	invent**ed**

LANGUAGE NOTES:

1. The past form is the same for all persons.
2. The verb after *to* does not use the past form.
   The Wright Brothers wanted *to fly*.
3. Spelling of the past tense of regular verbs:
   a. Add *–ed* or *–d* to most regular verbs: **start** ⟶ **started**   **live** ⟶ **lived**.
   b. When the base ends in consonant + *y*, change *y* to *i* and add *–ed*: **carry** ⟶ **carried**.
   c. When the base ends in vowel + *y*, do not change the *y*: **stay** ⟶ **stayed**.
   d. When a one-syllable verb ends in a C-V-C, double the final consonant + *–ed*:
      stop ⟶ **stopped**   **hug** ⟶ **hugged**.
   e. Do not double final *w* or *x*: **fix** ⟶ **fixed**   **show** ⟶ **showed**.
   f. When a two-syllable verb ends in a C-V-C, double the final consonant and add *–ed* only if the last syllable is stressed: **permít** ⟶ **permitted**.
   g. When the last syllable of a two-syllable verb is not stressed, do not double the final consonant: **ópen** ⟶ **opened**.

EXERCISE 1 Rewrite the sentences below, changing the verbs to the simple-past-tense verbs.

Example: I need a ticket. *I needed a ticket.*

1. I live in a small house. _____
2. We need money. _____
3. He starts school on Monday. _____
4. They offer me a ride. _____
5. Chris fixes my computer. _____
6. The tree moves in the wind. _____
7. The automatic doors will open. _____
8. Joanna looks out the window. _____
9. The cat cries at the door. _____
10. We open the presents. _____
11. She types her compositions. _____
12. We watch TV all day. _____

13. They drop the dishes. _____

14. The boys play soccer. _____

15. He permits games in class. _____

16. The teacher wants us to do well. _____

17. They paint pictures. _____

18. We travel to Tokyo. _____

EXERCISE 2 Write each sentence in the simple past tense.

Example: He (marry) _____ *married* _____ his sweetheart.

1. The doctor (treat) _____ her patients well.

2. We (try) _____ to listen to the instructions.

3. The girls (study) _____ their piano lessons.

4. The bus (arrive) _____ on time yesterday.

5. The landlord (rent) _____ the apartment last week.

6. Your friend (phone) _____ to say hello.

7. I (stop) _____ typing my composition two hours ago.

8. The woman (cancel) _____ her dentist appointment five minutes ago.

EXERCISE 3 Write six sentences about your childhood using the simple past tense. Use the verbs in the box.

Example: *I played with dolls.* _____

play	like	climb	enjoy	learn	start	want	need	live	move	watch
pretend	stay	jump	love	hate	use	decide	attend	visit	collect	

1. _____

2. _____

3. _____

4. _____

5. _____

6. _____

PRACTICE 40 Forms and Uses of the Past Tense of *Be*

SUBJECT	*BE*	*(NOT)*	COMPLEMENT
We	were		in New York.
Madame Curie	was		a scientist.
Gandhi and King	were	not	soldiers.
I	was	not	alone.

LANGUAGE NOTE: The contraction for *was not* is *wasn't*.
The contraction for *were not* is *weren't*.

EXAMPLE	EXPLANATION
Einstein was a scientist.	Classification of the subject
The soldiers were brave.	Description of the subject
The war was in Europe.	Location of the subject
The president was from Arkansas.	Place of origin of the subject
My sister was born in 1975.	With *born*
There were fireworks to celebrate the holiday last summer.	With *there*

EXERCISE 1 Write the way *be* is used in each of the sentences below: *classification, description, location,* or *origin.*

Example: The rug was on the floor. _____ *location* _____

1. Mitch was a salesman. _____
2. Leila was from Iran. _____
3. Mary and Fred were in Australia. _____
4. Her hat was lovely. _____
5. Gloria was hardworking. _____
6. Those flowers were from Daniel. _____
7. This book was interesting. _____
8. Kim was born in Korea. _____
9. The band was on tour. _____
10. It was an English school. _____

EXERCISE 2 Make the following sentences negative. Use negative contractions.

Example: The action film was wonderful.   _The action film wasn't wonderful._

1. The basketball games were exciting. _____
2. There were many excited fans. _____
3. The crowd was cheering. _____
4. The teams were well matched. _____
5. They were very skilled at free throws. _____
6. The point spread was even. _____
7. I was thrilled by the action. _____
8. We were sad to go home. _____

EXERCISE 3 Make sentences with the past tense of *be*. Some sentences will be negative.

Example: my teacher / very energetic   _My teacher was very energetic._

   our bosses / not / kind   _Our bosses weren't kind._

1. my friend / a singer _____
2. Manuel / so intelligent _____
3. my uncle / not / in California _____
4. they / from Haiti _____
5. there / a mouse in the kitchen _____
6. there / some books on the table _____
7. Joe and Michael / good athletes _____
8. I / not / a genius _____
9. my mother / tall _____
10. Ling / from the Philippines _____
11. Liz / not / a designer _____
12. you / not / in an airplane _____

EXERCISE 4 Think of a beautiful place you visited long ago. Write five sentences using *there was / were* to describe that place.

Example: _There was a forest with many tall trees._

1. _____
2. _____
3. _____
4. _____
5. _____

Questions with *Was* and *Were*

PRACTICE 41 Questions with *Was* and *Were*

WH–WORD	WAS / WERE	SUBJECT	WAS / WERE	COMPLEMENT	SHORT ANSWER
		The firefighters	were	concerned.	
	Were	the firefighters		concerned?	Yes, they were.
Why	were	the firefighters		concerned?	(No, they weren't.)
		The child	wasn't	alone.	
Why	wasn't	the child		alone?	
		Someone	was	with the child.	
		Who	was	with the child?	

EXERCISE 1 Read each statement. Then write a *yes / no* question with the words in parentheses ( ). Give a short answer.

Example: I was absent from class yesterday   (you)

Were you absent from class yesterday? _____   _No, I wasn't._ _____

1. The telephone was an important invention.   (the computer)

   _____   _____

2. Communication by e-mail is common now.   (50 years ago)

   _____   _____

3. You are working on your English now.   (yesterday)

   _____   _____

4. I was interested in animals when I was a child.   (you)

   _____   _____

5. I was on a soccer team in elementary school.   (you)

   _____   _____

6. I was tired yesterday.   (you)

   _____   _____

7. My first-grade teacher was nice.   (your first-grade teacher)

   _____   _____

8. My favorite toy was a stuffed chicken.   (your favorite toy)

   _____   _____

9. I was in a good mood yesterday. (you)

_____ _____

10. I was sick yesterday. (you)

_____ _____

EXERCISE 2 Read each statement. Then write a *wh–* question with the word in parentheses ( ).

Example: I was angry yesterday. (why)

Why were you angry yesterday? _____

1. She was in love. (why) _____
2. They were in the park. (when) _____
3. My sister was a student. (where) _____
4. His mother was curious. (why) _____
5. I was wearing a heavy coat. (why) _____
6. My parents were members of the club. (when) _____
7. I wasn't excited. (why) _____
8. You weren't nice to me. (when) _____
9. He was a director of the program. (when) _____
10. We weren't honest with the others. (why) _____

EXERCISE 3 Unscramble the words to form questions.

Example: sleepy / you / yesterday / were *Were you sleepy yesterday?* _____

1. born / you / were / where

   _____

2. on the first day / were / you / of class / nervous

   _____

3. you / were / a happy child

   _____

4. in English / were / interested / you / in elementary school

   _____

PRACTICE 42 Simple Past Tense of Irregular Verbs

VERBS WITH NO CHANGE		FINAL *D* CHANGES TO *T*	
bet–bet	let–let	bend–bent	send–sent
cost–cost	put–put	build–built	spend–spent
cut–cut	quit–quit	lend–lent	
fit–fit	shut–shut		
hit–hit			
hurt–hurt			

VERBS WITH A VOWEL OR CONSONANT CHANGE

feel–felt	lose–lost	bring–brought	fight–fought
keep–kept	mean–meant*	buy–bought	teach–taught
leave–left	sleep–slept	catch–caught	think–thought
break–broke	steal–stole	begin–began	sing–sang
freeze–froze	wake–woke	drink–drank	sink–sank
		ring–rang	swim–swam
dig–dug	spin–spun	drive–drove	shine–shone
hang–hung	win–won	ride–rode	write–wrote
blow–blew	grow–grew	bleed–bled	meet–met
draw–drew	know–knew	feed–fed	read–read**
fly–flew	throw–threw	lead–led	
sell–sold	tell–told	find–found	wind–wound
shake–shook	mistake–mistook	lay–laid	pay–paid
take–took		say–said***	
tear–tore	wear–wore	bite–bit	hide–hid
		light–lit	
become–became	eat–ate	fall–fell	hold–held
come–came			
give–gave	lie–lay	run–ran	see–saw
forgive–forgave		sit–sat	
forget–forgot	get–got	stand–stood	understand–understood
shoot–shot			

MISCELLANEOUS CHANGES

be–was / were	go–went		hear–heard
do–did	have–had		make–made

Meant sounds like *sent*.   **The past tense of *read* sounds like *red*.   ***Said* sounds like *bed*.

EXERCISE 1 Fill in the blank with the past tense form of the verb in parentheses.

Example: We (forget) _____ *forgot* _____ to bring our books today.

1. A dog (bite) _____ me yesterday.
2. Who (break) _____ the glass?
3. She (pay) _____ the waitress for her coffee.
4. I already (feed) _____ the cats.
5. Raisa (sing) _____ the most beautiful song.
6. Rain (fall) _____ all day yesterday.
7. Vito (buy) _____ a new watch.
8. My mother (teach) _____ English.
9. He only (sleep) _____ four hours last night.
10. Jim and Betty (ride) _____ the train from New York to Boston.
11. I (see) _____ a great movie last night.
12. Frances (go) _____ to Italy two years ago.
13. She never (forgive) _____ him for leaving her.
14. Fernando (make) _____ a cake for our party.
15. Do you remember what she (wear) _____?
16. She (keep) _____ the bracelet as a souvenir.
17. June and Henry always (fight) _____ .
18. He (say) _____ he will give us a ride home.
19. I (meet) _____ a very interesting person yesterday.
20. We (light) _____ candles and (hold) _____ hands.
21. Terry (speak) _____ very quietly.
22. Katya (find) _____ a dog in the park.
23. She (spin) _____ around until she felt sick.
24. Carola (lose) _____ her earring somewhere.
25. They (sell) _____ their house for a lot of money.
26. Alan (drive) _____ to work every day.
27. My new job (begin) _____ yesterday.
28. He (understand) _____ his new teacher perfectly.
29. Marcelo (choose) _____ a blue shirt to wear that day.
30. I (forget) _____ all the irregular verbs I learned last week.

EXERCISE 2 Write three sentences about the things that happened in your life last week. Use verbs from the chart at the beginning of this practice.

1. _____
2. _____
3. _____

Practice 42 **87**

PRACTICE 43 Negative Forms of Past Tense Verbs

AFFIRMATIVE STATEMENT	NEGATIVE STATEMENT
Ricardo **studied** history.	He **didn't study** mathematics.
He **became** a writer.	He **didn't become** a professor.
He **moved** to Oxford.	He **didn't move** to Cambridge.

LANGUAGE NOTE: For the negative of past tense verbs, use *didn't* *(did not)* + the base form for all verbs, regular and irregular.

EXERCISE 1   Fill in the blanks with the negative form of the underlined verb.

Example: He <u>thought</u> about the test.   He _____*didn't think*_____ about the time.

1.   I <u>bought</u> celery at the store. I _____ lettuce.

2.   We <u>ate</u> ice cream for dessert. We _____ fruit.

3.   I <u>thought</u> English was easy. I _____ about studying so much.

4.   Yesterday we <u>went</u> to the park. We _____ shopping.

5.   Neil <u>saw</u> a cloud. He _____ an airplane.

6.   I <u>won</u> second prize. Unfortunately, I _____ first prize.

7.   The thief <u>stole</u> our television, but he _____ our computer.

8.   Our teacher <u>taught</u> us history. He _____ us political science.

9.   I <u>fed</u> the birds at the park, but I _____ the squirrels.

10.   Mom <u>felt</u> tired yesterday. She _____ sick.

11.   Mr. Jones <u>drank</u> coffee. He _____ tea.

12.   Jeff <u>rode</u> his bicycle to school. He _____ the bus.

13.   I <u>knew</u> that English had irregular verbs, but I _____ how many!

14.   She <u>met</u> Bobby at the restaurant. She _____ him at the party.

15.   I <u>brought</u> a sweater, but I _____ a coat.

16.   They <u>made</u> some spaghetti. They _____ pizza.

17.   I <u>wrote</u> a long letter yesterday. I _____ my composition.

18.   I <u>grew</u> up in California. I _____ up in New York.

19.   Darla <u>had</u> a cold. She _____ the flu.

20.   Kit <u>ran</u> to school today. Kit _____ to school yesterday.

EXERCISE 2 Amy called to tell you about her coworkers and friends. These are the things that her friends *did* but she *didn't do.*

Example: Jill slept until 11 in the morning.   *I didn't sleep until 11 in the morning.*

1. Angel cut her hair last week. _____
2. Bob quit his job this week. _____
3. Cara caught a cold. _____
4. Darva woke at 4 a.m. _____
5. Eric chose some new plants. _____
6. Fred drove to Canada last month. _____
7. Helen swam in the ocean. _____
8. Irma fought with her sister. _____
9. Julio came to visit his mother. _____
10. Katie sat in the sun for one half hour. _____
11. Lee paid all his bills. _____
12. Michael shook out his rugs. _____
13. Peter did his laundry. _____
14. Soong Ye spoke to her family. _____

EXERCISE 3 What did Amy do yesterday? Choose the best verb to complete each sentence about her day.

Example: She _____*bought*_____ her mother a scarf at the new store.

hear draw get sick find stand bleed ring tear fall feel

Amy (1) _____ in the rain for two hours to wait for a

bus. When the bus came, she (2) _____ down on the sidewalk. She

(3) _____ the knee of her jeans. Her knee (4) _____

a little bit. After she stood up, she (5) _____ some money on the sidewalk.

Sadly, she (6) _____ sick from being wet and cold. From her

bed, she (7) _____ some great new music on the radio, and she

(8) _____ some pictures. The phone (9) _____ all

afternoon. All her friends called. They wanted to know if she (10) _____

better.

PRACTICE 44 Questions with Past Tense Verbs

WH–WORD	DID / DIDN'T	SUBJECT	VERB	COMPLEMENT	SHORT ANSWER
		Maria	**studied**	physics.	
	Did	she	**study**	hard?	Yes, she **did.**
Why	**did**	she	**study**	physics?	
		Peter	**flew**	to Japan.	
	Did	he	**fly**	alone?	Yes, he **did.**
When	**did**	he	**fly**	to Japan?	
Why	**didn't**	he	**fly**	with someone?	

LANGUAGE NOTES:

1. For all *yes / no* questions of past tense verbs, regular or irregular, we use *did* + the base form.
2. For most *wh–* questions, we use *did* + the base form.

 EXERCISE 1 Read each statement. Write a *yes / no* question about the words in the parentheses ( ).

Example: She had a cold. (a fever)

Did she have a fever?

1. We ate breakfast in the country. (outside)

   _____

2. I got my cousin Ada a present. (perfume)

   _____

3. He wrote several novels. (any plays)

   _____

4. Tomiko organized the meeting. (travel plans)

   _____

5. My mother bought a new car. (a red car)

   _____

6. George and Sophie had a baby. (a girl)

   _____

7. Carmen danced all night. (with Henry)

   _____

8. She worked on her homework. (composition)

9. Sigrid planted flowers.   (vegetables)

_____

10. Boris found a wallet yesterday.   (any money)

_____

EXERCISE 2 Complete the question based upon the answer given.

Example: What kind of engine _did the first airplane have?_ _____

    The first airplane had a gasoline engine.

1. Where _____

    We went to dinner at a nice restaurant.

2. Why _____

    I decided to study English because it is useful.

3. When _____

    This class started at 9:30.

4. Why _____

    He became a doctor because he wanted to help people.

5. Where _____

    I grew up in Stockholm.

6. When _____

    We got married three years ago.

7. Who _____

    Oh, I saw a lot of people at the conference.

8. When _____

    I got here about 10 minutes ago.

9. Why _____

    I didn't ask a question because I understood everything.

10. Why _____

    She didn't come with us because she had a date.

PRACTICE 45 Using Imperatives

EXAMPLE	USE
Get an application. **Print** your name on the first line. **Don't print** your name on the bottom line.	To give instructions
Please **show** me your driver's license. **Take** this card to the front desk, please.	To make a request
Don't open my mail. **Stand** at attention! **Don't be** late.	To make a command
Watch out! **Be** careful! **Don't** move! You're under arrest.	To give a warning
Have a nice day. **Make** yourself at home. **Drive** safely.	In certain polite conversational expressions
Mind your own business!	In some angry, impolite expressions

LANGUAGE NOTES:

1. To form the imperative, we use the base form. The subject of the imperative is *you*, but we don't include *you* in the sentence.
2. A negative imperative is *do not* + base form. The contraction is *don't*.
3. An exclamation point (!) is used to show strong emotion.

EXERCISE 1 Explain the use of these imperatives. Choose one for each.

Example: Wait for me! *B. To make a request*

A. To give instructions	B. To make a request	C. To make a command
D. To give a warning	E. In polite conversation	F. In impolite expression

1. Don't waste time. _____

2. Take care of yourself. _____

3. Be quiet! _____

4. Open the door. _____

5. Steady now! _____

6. Relax and stay a while. _____

7. Be good! _____

8. Take out your books. _____

9. Please tell me the way to the post office. _____

10. Stop where you are! _____

11. Please don't worry about it. _____

12. Get away from me! _____

13. Turn to page 9 in the book. _____

14. Take your time. _____

EXERCISE 2 Fill in each blank with an appropriate imperative verb (affirmative or negative) to give instructions on how to be a good language learner.

Example: _Practice_ _____ your pronunciation.

1. _____ questions.

2. _____ with native speakers.

3. _____ your homework.

4. _____ be absent.

5. _____ your textbook.

6. _____ your notebook.

7. _____ notes.

8. _____ to your teacher.

9. _____ in class.

10. _____ your best.

EXERCISE 3 Fill in each blank with an appropriate imperative verb (affirmative or negative) to give instructions on how to behave in a job interview.

Example: _Don't wear_ _____ strange clothes.

1. _____ late.

2. _____ nice clothes.

3. _____ your résumé.

4. _____ a pen to fill out the application.

5. _____ gum.

6. _____ the interviewer's questions.

7. _____ to smile.

8. _____ politely.

PRACTICE 46 Verbs Followed by an Infinitive

SUBJECT	VERB	INFINITIVE	COMPLEMENT
I	want	**to get**	the best price.
The salesperson	hopes	**to make**	a sale.
We	are planning	**to buy**	a new TV.

LANGUAGE NOTES:

1. An infinitive is *to* + the base form of a verb.
2. We often use an infinitive after the following verbs:

begin	expect	like	plan	start
continue	forget	love	prefer	try
decide	hope	need	promise	want

3. An infinitive never has an ending. It never shows the tense. Only the first verb shows the tense.

EXERCISE 1 Circle the correct verb.

Example: I love try / (to try) on new clothes.

1. I begin to think / thought about that show.

2. The teacher tries explain / to explain the grammar.

3. The children to promise / promise to be good.

4. The doctor need / needs to see the patients.

5. You like to have / had new adventures, don't you?

6. I expect to / to expect to see your family someday soon.

7. They continue to love / love to their baseball team.

8. She started to get / get a head cold.

9. My mother prefers / prefer herbal tea.

10. We all wanting / want to go on a vacation.

11. He hopes to lose / losing weight for his health.

12. I forgot call him / to call him last night.

13. They need driving / to drive my friend home now.

14. My father doesn't want to go / going on a boat trip.

15. I love to be / to being inside on a rainy day.

16. She began to felt / to feel better after one day.

EXERCISE 2 Unscramble the words. Then give a short answer with information about yourself.

Example: want / buy / new car

Do you want to buy a new car? _____   *No, I don't.* _____

1.   like / sweets / you / eat / to / do

_____   _____

2.   try / you / exercise / every day / to / do

_____   _____

3.   do / want / on a vacation / go / you / to

_____   _____

4.   to / you / do / plan / get married / soon

_____   _____

5.   expect / use / English / in the future / to / do / you

_____   _____

EXERCISE 3 Make a sentence with the words given.

Example: I / like / play   *I like to play the Spanish guitar.* _____

1.   I / like / listen to   _____

2.   she / love / go   _____

3.   he / try / learn   _____

4.   you / want / buy   _____

5.   we / need / find   _____

6.   I / hope / finish   _____

7.   they / continue / practice   _____

8.   I / try / think   _____

9.   we / begin / like   _____

10.   you / not / prefer / eat   _____

11.   my friend / want / try   _____

12.   he / decide / learn   _____

PRACTICE 47 It + Be + Adjective + Infinitive / Be + Adjective + Infinitive

IT	BE (+ NOT)	ADJECTIVE	INFINITIVE PHRASE
It	is	important	**to save** your receipt.
It	isn't	necessary	**to go back** to the first store.
It	was	easy	**to shop.**

LANGUAGE NOTE: We can use an infinitive after the following adjectives:

dangerous	good	possible	expensive
difficult	hard	necessary	impossible
easy	important	fun	

SUBJECT	BE	ADJECTIVE	INFINITIVE PHRASE
I	am	happy	**to call** the other store.
You	are	lucky	**to have** a job.
She	wasn't	ready	**to buy** a new TV.

LANGUAGE NOTE: We can use an infinitive after the following adjectives:

afraid	happy	prepared	ready
glad	lucky	proud	sad

EXERCISE 1 Match each statement with a related infinitive phrase. More than one answer is correct.

Example: It's easy ⟶ to talk to my friends.

1. It's dangerous — to spell.
2. It's good — to know the future.
3. It isn't possible — to find a fast-food restaurant.
4. It's expensive — to learn new video games.
5. It's difficult — to keep your door locked at night.
6. It wasn't hard — to find a cheap hotel room in this city.
7. It was impossible — to walk home in the dark.
8. It's easy — to spell English words.
9. It isn't easy — to buy designer shoes and bags.
10. It's important — to go dancing.
11. It's fun — to leave your bag in the library.
12. It was dangerous — to ask for help.

EXERCISE 2   Complete each statement with an infinitive phrase.

Example: It isn't difficult *to learn English.*

1.   It's impossible   _____
2.   It's possible   _____
3.   It's necessary   _____
4.   It isn't necessary   _____
5.   It's expensive   _____
6.   It isn't difficult   _____
7.   It's easy   _____
8.   It's important   _____
9.   It's dangerous   _____
10.   It's fun   _____
11.   It isn't hard   _____
12.   It's good   _____

EXERCISE 3   Complete each statement with a subject + *be* verb form + adjective.

Example: to be here today   *I'm happy to be here today.*

I'm proud	I'm lucky	I'm happy	I'm afraid	I'm prepared
I'm ready	I'm sad	I'm nervous	I'm glad	I'm thrilled

1.   to take the big math exam   _____
2.   to respect my cultural heritage   _____
3.   to meet you   _____
4.   to meet the future   _____
5.   to drive on the highway at night   _____
6.   to know people like you   _____
7.   to speak a new language   _____
8.   to win the lottery   _____
9.   to lose contact with old friends   _____
10.   to go home   _____

PRACTICE 48 Using the Infinitive to Show Purpose

EXAMPLE	EXPLANATION
I went to the store **to buy** a VCR. I bought a VCR **to record** my favorite programs. The saleswoman called another store **to check** the price.	We use the infinitive to show the purpose of an action. We can also say *in order to:* I bought a VCR **in order to** record my favorite programs.

EXERCISE 1 Answer each question with an infinitive phrase to show purpose.

Example: Why did you buy a cell phone?   *To call my friends.*

1.   Why do you use a toothbrush?   _____

2.   What do you use a computer for?   _____

3.   Why did she go to the supermarket?   _____

4.   Why do people go to discos?   _____

5.   Why do you need a pencil?   _____

6.   Why will you buy a car?   _____

7.   Why did you go to the shopping mall?   _____

8.   Why did he buy a camera?   _____

9.   Why did they go to the post office?   _____

10.   Why do you practice grammar?   _____

11.   Why do people take vitamins?   _____

12.   Why did they move to the city?   _____

13.   Why do people use credit cards?   _____

14.   Why did you buy this textbook?   _____

15.   Why do people take vacations?   _____

Answer these questions with information about yourself and other people. Use the infinitive to show purpose. Write complete sentences.

Example: Why are you using eyeglasses?   *I'm using eyeglasses to read better.*

1. Why are you studying English?

   _____

2. Why did you decide to come to this school?

   _____

3. What do you use your dictionary for?

   _____

4. Why do you think people go to other countries?

   _____

5. Why do people go on diets?

   _____

6. What do people use computers for?

   _____

7. Why do people go to the beach?

   _____

8. What can you use a cassette tape recorder for?

   _____

9. What do you need a bag for?

   _____

10. How do you use your free time?

    _____

11. Why do people use makeup?

    _____

12. Why do you use a dictionary?

    _____

Using the Infinitive to Show Purpose

PRACTICE 49 Overview of Modals

LIST OF MODALS	FACTS ABOUT MODALS
can **could** **should** **will** **would** **may** **might** **must** (have to) (be able to)	1. Modals are different from other verbs because they don't take an *–s*, *–ed*, or *–ing* ending: He **can** drive. (**not:** He **cans** drive.) 2. Modals are different from other verbs because we don't use an infinitive after a modal. We use the base form. Compare: He wants **to leave**. He **must leave**. 3. To form the negative, put *not* after the modal. He **should not** drive. 4. Some verbs are like modals in meaning: *have to, be able to:* He **can** pay the rent = He **is able to** pay the rent.

WH- WORD	MODAL (+ *NOT*)	SUBJECT	MODAL (+ *NOT*)	MAIN VERB	COMPLEMENT	SHORT ANSWER
		Mario	**should**	study	English.	
		He	**shouldn't**	study	literature.	
	Should	he		study	grammar?	Yes, he **should.**
Why	**should**	he		study	grammar?	
Why	**shouldn't**	he		study	literature?	
		Who	**should**	study	literature?	

EXERCISE 1 Underline the modals in the sentences below.

Example: You <u>must</u> be here by 9:00.

1. We shouldn't talk in class.
2. Do you have to play the music so loud?
3. I can write with my left hand.
4. I can understand French.
5. She might go tomorrow.
6. Why would we do this now?
7. There should be a sign somewhere.
8. We must turn left soon.

9. May we leave early today?

10. I should take an aspirin.

EXERCISE 2 Unscramble these words to write statements.

Example: drive / she / can't   _She can't drive._ _____

1. he / pen / can / use / a   _____
2. she / eat / her / should / dinner   _____
3. can't / they / swim   _____
4. leave / Gloria / apartment / might / her   _____
5. he / come / on Friday / may   _____
6. do / it / you / could / in the morning   _____
7. you / taking / will / be / notes   _____
8. wouldn't / me / Alan / the secret / tell   _____
9. my / may / mother / be / there   _____
10. you / listen / me / to / must   _____

EXERCISE 3 Unscramble these words to make questions.

Example: drive / she / can't   _Can't she drive?_ _____

1. can / Spanish / you / speak   _____
2. will / he / us / meet / there   _____
3. should / I / buy / one   _____
4. you / talk / must / so loudly   _____
5. could / I / water / glass / of / have / a   _____
6. pass / me / would / you / the / please / butter   _____
7. sing / Marianne / can   _____
8. the concert / with / couldn't / us / he / go / to   _____
9. leave / a / shouldn't / we / tip   _____
10. a store / won't / there / be / there   _____

PRACTICE **50**   *Can* and *Should*

EXAMPLE	EXPLANATION
I **can** drive.	Ability
If you go to discount stores, you **can** save money.	Possibility
The sign says "Parking on Weekdays Only." You **can** park here only Monday through Friday.	Permission

LANGUAGE NOTE: The negative of *can* is *cannot* (one word). The contraction is *can't*.

EXAMPLE	EXPLANATION
You **should** try it on before you buy it.	Advice
You **should not** drink it.	Warning

LANGUAGE NOTE: The negative of *should* is *should not*. The contraction is *shouldn't*.

EXERCISE 1   Fill in each blank with *can* or *can't* to tell about your abilities.

Example: I ___*can't*___ play the piano.

1. I _____ speak two languages.
2. I _____ run fast.
3. I _____ swim.
4. I _____ use a computer.
5. I _____ cook.

6. I _____ play an instrument.
7. I _____ ride a motorcycle.
8. I _____ ride a bicycle.
9. I _____ write with my left hand.
10. I _____ sing opera.

EXERCISE 2   Underline the modal and label the purpose of the modal in each sentence. For *can*, use *ability, possibility,* or *permission*. For *should,* use *advice* or *warning*.

Example: You <u>can't</u> chew gum in class.   ___*permission*___

1. She can operate heavy machinery.   _____
2. He should drive more carefully.   _____
3. You should slow down when driving.   _____
4. You should never eat from a punctured can.   _____
5. We can try to work together.   _____
6. They can speak many languages.   _____
7. No one should walk in the street.   _____

8. You should stop eating salt or you will be ill. _____

9. You can get extra help on Wednesday. _____

10. We can come visit you next week. _____

EXERCISE 3 What should the person do in each of the following situations? Write a sentence of advice using *should* for each situation.

Example: He lost his wallet. *He should report it to the police.*

1. She is tired. _____

2. He needs money. _____

3. She has a cold. _____

4. She wants a new dress. _____

5. His CD player is broken. _____

EXERCISE 4 What warning would you give a person in each of the following situations?

Example: The car is too expensive. *You shouldn't buy it.*

1. The coffee is very hot. _____

2. The test is difficult. _____

3. The roads are covered with ice. _____

4. The neighborhood is dangerous. _____

5. That dog bites. _____

EXERCISE 5 What *can* and *can't* students do in your class? Fill in the blanks.

Example: We _____ *can't* _____ listen to headphones.

1. We _____ talk with our friends.
2. We _____ use pencils.
3. We _____ eat.
4. We _____ sleep.
5. We _____ speak our native language.

6. We _____ take notes.
7. We _____ bring our pets.
8. We _____ wear hats.
9. We _____ wear sneakers.
10. We _____ dance.

PRACTICE 51 *Must, and Must versus Have To*

EXAMPLE	EXPLANATION
You **must** finish your composition by Friday.	Rules
A driver **must** stop at a red light.	Laws
You **must not** eat on the bus.	Prohibition

LANGUAGE NOTE: The contraction for *must not* is *mustn't*.

EXAMPLE		EXPLANATION
Affirmative	You **must** use a coupon by a certain date.	It is a rule.
	You **have to** use a coupon by a certain date	
	I have to buy groceries tomorrow.	It is a personal obligation or necessity.
Negative	You **must not** steal.	It is against the law.
	If a sale sign says, "3 for $1.00," you **don't have to** buy three items.	It's not necessary to buy three items to get the sale price.

LANGUAGE NOTES:

1. In affirmative statements, *have to* and *must* are very similar in meaning. They both show necessity. *Have to* is more common than *must* with a personal necessity or obligation. Must is stronger and usually tells about the rules:

    I *have to* go to the bank today.

    I *must* go to court next week.

2. In negative statements, *must* and *have to* are very different. *Must not* shows that something is prohibited, against the rules: *Don't / doesn't have to* shows that something is not necessary to:

    You *must not* drive without a license.

    I *don't have to* drive to school. I can walk.

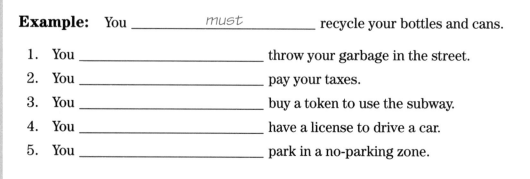

EXERCISE 1 Fill in each blank with *must* or *must not* to tell about laws in your city.

Example: You _____*must*_____ recycle your bottles and cans.

1. You _____ throw your garbage in the street.

2. You _____ pay your taxes.

3. You _____ buy a token to use the subway.

4. You _____ have a license to drive a car.

5. You _____ park in a no-parking zone.

EXERCISE 2 Fill in each blank with *have to* or *don't have to* to make true statements about your schedule. Remember that *don't have to* means *not necessary to*.

Example: I ___*have to*___ go to the post office today.

1. I _____ meet someone today.
2. I _____ make a call later.
3. I _____ wash the dishes now.
4. I _____ do laundry this week.
5. I _____ clean my room later.
6. I _____ write a composition.
7. I _____ take a test in this class this week.
8. I _____ go grocery shopping tomorrow.
9. I _____ work today.
10. I _____ exercise today.

EXERCISE 3 Fill in each blank with a verb to tell what these people have to or don't have to do in these situations.

Example: My cat is hungry. I have to _____*feed*_____ it.

1. Martha's car is dirty. She has to _____ it.
2. Joseph is on vacation. He doesn't have to _____.
3. Alberto needs money. He must _____ a job.
4. Val and Henry are rich. They don't have to _____.
5. Sarah is a teacher. She must _____ homework to her students.
6. David is a student. He has to _____.
7. The party is casual. You don't have to _____.
8. I have a job interview tomorrow. I have to _____ a suit.
9. Katherine found someone's bag. She has to _____ it.
10. The teacher collected our compositions. He has to _____ them.
11. They are diabetic. They must not _____ sugar.
12. You drive a car. You must _____ an updated license.
13. He missed six classes already. He must not _____ another class.
14. The assignment was optional. You don't have to _____ it.
15. To prevent injury, all children must _____ seatbelts in a car.

PRACTICE **52** *Might, May, and Will*

EXAMPLE	EXPLANATION
I **may** go out for dinner tonight. I **might** have Chinese food. I **may** go to Europe in the fall. If you don't study, you **might** fail.	*May* and *might* have the same meaning. They show possibility.
I **will** go to a movie tonight. I **will** meet my friends. I **will** go to Florida next month.	*Will* shows certainty about the future.

EXERCISE 1 Fill in each blank with a verb to express what *may* or *might* happen or be true.

Example: It is cloudy today. It might _____ *rain* _____ this afternoon.

1. The baby is playing with a coin. She might _____ it.
2. The dog is barking a lot. It might _____ hungry.
3. I don't know what we are going to do tonight. We may _____ home.
4. Mom's upstairs working. She might _____ the phone.
5. Kenny's forehead feels hot. He may _____ a fever.
6. George is a half an hour late. He might _____ lost.
7. Carol went out. She may _____ at the store.
8. This is a no-parking zone. We may _____ a ticket.
9. I need a present for Charles. I might _____ him a CD player.
10. I may _____ my friend at the movie theater later.

EXERCISE 2 Write what *may* or *might* happen in the following situations.

Example: If you get a new job, *you might make more money.* _____

1. If you come to class every day, _____
2. If you make too much noise in your apartment, _____
3. If you smile at someone on the street, _____

4. If you go to a foreign country, _____

5. If you never practice English, _____

6. If you eat very healthy foods, _____

7. If you meet and fall in love, _____

8. If you move to a different city, _____

9. If you go shopping this weekend, _____

10. If you eat too many sweets, _____

 EXERCISE 3 Fill in each blank with *may, might, will, may not, might not,* or *won't* to make true statements about your future.

Example: I _____*might not*_____ get married.

1. I _____ have many (more) children.

2. I _____ get a (new) job.

3. I _____ live in another country.

4. I _____ retire early.

5. I _____ be very successful.

6. I _____ write a book.

7. I _____ make a movie.

8. I _____ travel around the world.

9. I _____ learn another language.

10. I _____ become famous.

EXERCISE 4 Complete these sentences.

1. Next year I may _____

2. In a month I might _____

3. Tomorrow I will _____

4. Tonight I may not _____

5. Today I might not _____

6. This year I won't _____

TO REQUEST	EXPLANATION
Would } you cash my check please? Could	These expressions are more polite than "Cash my check."

TO ASK PERMISSION	EXPLANATION
May Could } I use your pen please? Can	These expressions are more polite than "Give me your pen."

TO EXPRESS DESIRE	EXPLANATION
I **would like** to cash a check. How **would** you **like** your change?	*Would like* has the same meaning as *want*. *Would like* is softer than *want*. The contraction of would after a pronoun is **'d**: *I'd like* to cash a check.

LANGUAGE NOTES:

1. A command is very strong and is impolite in some situations. It is softer and more polite to use modals to make a request:

   Give me my journal. **versus** May I have my journal?

2. Some people consider *may I . . . ?* more polite than *can I . . . ?* for permission.

EXERCISE 1 Read the following conversation between a hairdresser (H) and a customer (C). Change the underlined words in each sentence to make the sentence more polite. Change periods to question marks where necessary.

Example: <u>Do you want</u> your hair cut?

Would you like your hair cut?

H: What kind of haircut (1) <u>do you want</u>? 1. _____

C: (2) I <u>want</u> a trim. 2. _____

   (3) <u>Cut</u> the ends a little. 3. _____

   And (4) <u>make</u> it a bit shorter in the front. 4. _____

H: All right. (5) <u>Do you want</u> a magazine? 5. _____

C: Yes. (6) <u>Bring</u> me *Vogue* if you have it. 6. _____

H: (7) <u>Sit back</u> a little. 7. _____

   I (8) <u>want</u> to shampoo your hair first. 8. _____

C: (9) <u>Use</u> warmer water. 9. _____

H: Sure. (10) <u>Do you want</u> to color your
hair too today?   10. _____

C: Yes. (11) <u>Make</u> it darker.   11. _____

H: Look at these color samples.
Which color (12) <u>do you want</u>?   12. _____

C: (13) <u>Mix</u> these two colors.   13. _____

H: Mmm hmm. (14) <u>Do you want</u> anything
to drink? We have tea, coffee, and
spring water.   14. _____

C: I (15) <u>want</u> spring water.   15. _____

H: (16) <u>Wait</u> just a moment.   16. _____

EXERCISE 2 Write what you would say in the following situations in your class.

Examples: You want someone to spell a word for you.
Could you spell this, please?

You want to borrow some money.
May I borrow 5 dollars until tomorrow?

1. You want your teacher to repeat something.

   _____

2. You want your teacher to speak more slowly.

   _____

3. You want your teacher to speak louder.

   _____

4. You want your teacher to explain something.

   _____

5. You want to ask a question.

   _____

6. You want to borrow some paper from a classmate.

   _____

7. You want to use someone's dictionary.

   _____

8. You want to borrow someone's eraser.

   _____

9. You want a noisy classmate to be quiet.

   _____

10. You want to join someone's group.

   _____

PRACTICE 54 Noncount Nouns

There are several types of noncount nouns as described below.

GROUP A: Nouns that have no distinct separate parts. We look at the whole.

milk	yogurt	soup
oil	air	bread
water	pork	meat
coffee	cholesterol	butter

GROUP B: Nouns that have parts that are too small or insignificant to count.

rice	snow	hair
sugar	sand	grass
salt	corn	popcorn

GROUP C: Nouns that are classes or categories of things. The members of the category are not the same.

money (nickels, dimes, dollars)	**mail** (letters, packages, postcards)
food (vegetables, meat, spaghetti)	**fruit** (cherries, apples, grapes)
furniture (chairs, tables, beds)	**makeup** (lipstick, rouge, eye shadow)
clothing (sweaters, pants, dresses)	**candy** (chocolates, candy bars, hard candies)

GROUP D: Nouns that are abstractions.

love	beauty	advice	information	happiness	music
life	luck	knowledge	noise	education	art
time	fun	nutrition	intelligence	experience	crime
truth		unemployment		work	

EXERCISE 1 Label each noun *count* or *noncount*.

Example: water ___noncount___

1. teacher _____
2. paper _____
3. silence _____
4. truck _____
5. wind _____
6. light _____
7. joy _____
8. calendar _____

9. soda _____
10. building _____
11. syrup _____
12. shoe _____
13. flower _____
14. mail _____
15. soup _____
16. rain _____

EXERCISE 2 Fill in each blank with a noncount noun.

Example: I want a better job, so I need more _education._

1. He ate a lot of _____, especially bananas and strawberries.
2. In South American countries, people eat a lot of beans and _____.
3. Many children like sweet foods such as _____ and cake.
4. The _____ in the yard is so green this year.
5. There is too much _____ in most sodas.
6. I'd love to see you this week, but I don't have _____.
7. She wore a lot of _____—bright red lipstick and black eyeliner.
8. Our office uses so much _____. I hate to kill all those trees.
9. Is there any _____ in the kettle? I want to make some _____.
10. There's too much _____ in here. I can't hear what you're saying.
11. I respect my teacher. She has so much _____ about English grammar.
12. How much _____ do you have with you? I only have 10 dollars.
13. I'd like some _____ about trips to the Middle East. I want to go there soon.
14. OK everyone, get busy. There's a lot of _____ to do around here.
15. When I am mayor, I promise to reduce _____. I promise to make this city safe.
16. Did you do all your _____ last night? I didn't finish my composition.
17. Let's not go grocery shopping. We have a lot of _____ in the refrigerator.
18. I went to the beach last week, and I still have _____ in my shoes.
19. Look at all that _____! Let's go skiing!
20. Let me give you some _____: If you want to learn a language, you have to practice, practice, practice!

EXERCISE 3 Answer these questions using some of the noncount nouns from the chart at the beginning of this practice.

Example: What do you look for in a girlfriend?
I look for patience, intelligence, and beauty.

1. What do you need to make a cake?

   _____

2. What are the most important things in life?

   _____

3. What are our basic needs?

   _____

4. What are some problems in big cities today?

   _____

PRACTICE 55 — A Lot of, Much, and Many

	COUNT (PLURAL)	NONCOUNT
Affirmative	He baked **many** cookies.	He baked **a lot of** bread.
	He baked **a lot of** cookies.	
Negative	He didn't bake **many** cookies.	He didn't bake **much** bread.
	He didn't bake **a lot of** cookies.	He didn't bake **a lot of** bread.
Question	Did he bake **many** cookies?	Did he bake **much** bread?
	Did he bake **a lot of** cookies?	Did he bake **a lot of** bread?
	How **many** cookies did he bake?	How **much** bread did he bake?

LANGUAGE NOTES:

1. We rarely use *much* in affirmative statements. We usually use it with questions and negatives. In affirmative statements, we use *a lot of*:
   Did he drink *much* coffee? No, he didn't drink *much* coffee. He drank *a lot of* water.
2. When the noun is omitted, we say *a lot*, not *a lot of*:
   Did he bake *a lot* of bread? No, he didn't bake *a lot*.

EXERCISE 1 Fill in each blank with *much*, *many*, or *a lot of*. In some cases, more than one answer is possible.

Example: I bought ___*a lot of*___ food yesterday.

1. I don't have _____ money with me today.
2. Is there _____ sugar in the cake?
3. _____ people think she's a good singer.
4. How _____ minutes are there in an hour?
5. How _____ time do we have?
6. There are _____ magazines in the living room.
7. Did he read _____ books on vacation?
8. We didn't have _____ good experiences there.
9. I have _____ jewelry.
10. There isn't _____ oil in this dish.
11. I saw _____ movies last month.
12. I don't have _____ friends.
13. Does he have _____ cars?
14. They don't have _____ candy left.
15. Did you see _____ interesting birds?
16. There are _____ kinds of flowers.

17. How _____ times have you seen this show?

18. How _____ work will it take to finish the project?

19. I don't have _____ books.

20. How _____ pairs of socks do you have?

21. Is there _____ snow outside?

22. There's not _____ snow, but there's a lot of ice.

23. My little sister has _____ toys.

24. I had _____ comic books when I was little.

25. He doesn't eat _____ food.

EXERCISE 2 Write questions asking how much someone has. Make questions using *much, many,* or *a lot of.*

Example: (you / books) *Do you have a lot of books?* _____

1. (he / free time) _____

2. (they / friends) _____

3. (she / homework) _____

4. (store / clothes) _____

5. (your friend / jewelry) _____

6. (he / job experience) _____

7. (you / anger) _____

8. (she / relatives) _____

9. (we / patience) _____

10. (they / CDs) _____

EXERCISE 3 Answer the questions in Exercise 2 with short answers. Use *a lot of, much,* or *many.*

Example: Do you have many photographs of your trip? *Yes, I have many photographs.*

1. _____   6. _____

2. _____   7. _____

3. _____   8. _____

4. _____   9. _____

5. _____   10. _____

A Few, A Little, Some, Any, A, and An

	SINGULAR COUNT	PLURAL COUNT	NONCOUNT
Affirmative	I ate *a* banana.	I ate *a few* bananas.	I spent *a little* money.
	I ate *an* apple.	I ate *some* grapes.	I ate *some* rice.
Negative	I didn't eat *an* apple.	I didn't eat *any* grapes.	I didn't eat *any* rice.
Question	Did you eat *an* apple?	Did you eat *any* grapes?	Did you eat *any* rice?

LANGUAGE NOTES:

1. We use *some* in questions when we expect an affirmative answer (such as with requests and offers):

   Do you want *some* fruit?

2. We use *any* with questions and negative statements.

EXERCISE 1 Fill in each blank with *a few* or *a little*.

Examples: Could I have _____*a little*_____ more time?

He has _____*a few*_____ pencils in his bag.

1. There is _____ cream in my coffee.

2. _____ students in my class are married.

3. I have _____ good CDs at home.

4. We have _____ extra time today.

5. He has _____ knowledge on the subject.

6. Can you lend me _____ dollars?

7. I need _____ more minutes.

8. Could you put _____ salt on this?

9. I'd like _____ more rice.

10. There are _____ things I'd like to talk to you about.

11. She has _____ really good friends.

12. Aren't there _____ eggs in the refrigerator?

13. First, put _____ oil in a pan.

14. She wants a ring with _____ diamonds in it.

15. Show her _____ appreciation!

16. He has _____ more work to do.

17. They have _____ children.

18. There are _____ new words in this reading.

19. I still have _____ hope.

20. You need _____ patience to learn a language.

21. Jorge has _____ compositions to finish before he can pass the class.

22. I have _____ money. Let's buy _____ cookies.

23. Every day we learn _____ new grammar structures.

24. There are _____ movies I really want to see.

25. I'd like _____ coffee, please.

EXERCISE 2 Fill in each blank with *a, an, some,* or *any.*

Example: Do you have _____*any*_____ cheese?

1. Would you like _____ tea?

2. Can I have _____ juice?

3. There's _____ bread on the counter.

4. Could you get me _____ onion?

5. Do you have _____ tomatoes?

6. We need _____ flowers.

7. Do you have _____ sharp knife?

8. Is there _____ pepper?

9. Did you buy _____ spaghetti?

10. I want _____ glass of milk.

11. Are there _____ large bags?

12. Do you have _____ can opener?

13. There's _____ garlic in the salad.

14. There isn't _____ cheese.

15. Let's add _____ pepper.

16. This needs _____ salt.

17. There aren't _____ clean dishes!

18. I'll wash _____ dishes, then.

19. Are there _____ napkins?

20. Here's _____ olive oil.

21. I'll cut _____ carrots.

22. Here's _____ fresh head of lettuce.

23. Would you like _____ more sauce?

24. Let's invite _____ friends over for dinner.

25. She needs _____ cooking lessons.

26. He watched _____ great chef on TV.

27. He mixed up _____ salad dressing.

28. Did you want _____ soup?

29. Did he eat _____ spinach?

30. I drank _____ cup of tea.

31. They drank _____ lemonade.

32. Did you give the cook _____ credit?

33. She doesn't need _____ advice.

34. _____ encouragement can go a long way.

PRACTICE 57 Adjectives

EXAMPLE	EXPLANATION
My sister has a **healthy** baby. Her son is **active.** His hair is **curly** and **brown.**	Adjectives describe nouns.
Nancy is a **good** friend. I have many **good** friends.	Adjectives are always singular.
Today is a **beautiful, warm** day.	Sometimes we put two adjectives before a noun. We sometimes separate the adjectives with a comma.
You have a **blue** bag. I have a **green** <u>one</u>. We had an **interesting** class. We didn't have a **boring** <u>one</u>. Do you like **romantic** movies or **scary** <u>ones</u>?	After an adjective, we can substitute a singular count noun with *one* and a plural count noun with *ones*.
Do you prefer **hot** tea or **iced?** I prefer **iced.**	In questions and answers about choice, use the adjective alone with noncount nouns.

LANGUAGE NOTES:
1. We use adjectives before nouns or after the verbs *be, become, look, seem,* and other sense perception verbs.
2. Some *–ed* words are adjectives: marri*ed*, excit*ed*, frustrat*ed*, worri*ed*, crowd*ed*, or bor*ed*.

EXERCISE 1 Fill in each blank with an appropriate adjective. Change *a* to *an* if the adjective begins with a vowel.

Example: This is a_n interesting_ class.

1. My room is _____ .
2. I live in a _____ city.
3. I like _____ movies.
4. My clothes are _____ .
5. I am a _____ person.
6. I am a _____ student.
7. I like _____ food.
8. I come from a _____ country.
9. My parents are _____ .
10. My teacher is _____ .

11. My best friend is _____ .

12. The sky looks _____ today.

13. I am not _____ .

14. I am feeling _____ .

EXERCISE 2 Write a question of preference with the words given. Use *one* or *ones* to substitute for the count noun. Use the adjective alone for the noncount noun. Follow the example. Then write a short answer.

Example: funny movies / serious

Do you prefer funny movies or serious ones?

I prefer funny ones.

sunny weather / rainy

Do you prefer sunny weather or rainy?

I prefer sunny.

1. long hair / short

   _____

   _____

2. big families / small

   _____

   _____

3. a modern house / old

   _____

   _____

4. short, difficult tests / long, easy

   _____

   _____

5. a happy but poor life / unhappy but rich

   _____

   _____

6. fast-paced, action movie / romantic

   _____

   _____

7. cheap used car / new expensive

   _____

   _____

PRACTICE 58 Noun Modifiers

NOUN + NOUN	EXPLANATION
She had a **college** education. She wrote her **life** story.	We sometimes use a noun to describe another noun.

LANGUAGE NOTES:

1. When two nouns come together, the second noun is more general than the first:
   A department store is a store.
2. When two nouns come together, the first is always singular:
   A rose garden is a garden of roses.
3. Sometimes we write the two nouns separately:
   orange juice   desk lamp   vegetable garden
4. Sometimes we write the two nouns as one word:
   flashlight   ashtray   motorcycle

EXERCISE 1   Fill in each blank by putting the two nouns in the correct order. Remember to take the *s* off plural nouns. If we write the noun modifier as one word, you will see an asterisk (*).

Example: I want a (vegetables / garden) *vegetable garden* _____.

1. This is my favorite (show / television) _____.

2. Which (computer / game) _____ do you like best?

3. The (videos / store) _____ is near here.

4. Do you want to watch a (horror / movie) _____?

5. She's wearing a (necklace / pearls) _____.

6. She also has on a (diamonds / ring) _____.

7. I need a (wool / coat) _____.

8. I got you a (*plant / house) _____.

9. There's a new (*light / bulb) _____ in the cabinet.

10. Does he wear (*eyes / glasses) _____?

11. Mimi's a (cat / house) _____.

12. I can't find my (*brush / hair) _____!

13. I wish I could travel in a (time / machine) _____.

14. This is such a useful (book / grammar) _____.

15. I made this from an (eggs / carton) _____.

16. This is my favorite (box / music) _____.

17. My little sister is in (nursery / school) _____.
18. I love the decoration in this (window / shop) _____.
19. Just throw it in the (*can / trash) _____.
20. I can't wait until (vacation / spring) _____.
21. I want to plant a (garden / flowers) _____.
22. He wants to open a (coffee / shop) _____.
23. I think it's on the (dinner / table) _____.
24. We need a good (roads / map) _____.
25. Watch out! There's a (stop / sign) _____!
26. Can you feel that beautiful (breeze / ocean) _____?
27. My mom's a (expert / computers) _____.
28. Can I have some more (cream / ice) _____?
29. You will find the grammar textbook in the (*book / case).
30. Check our route on the (map / road) _____.
31. I'll drive you to the (station / train) _____.
32. Put the food on the (table / dinner) _____.

EXERCISE 2 Answer each of the following questions with one noun-modified word.

Example: What is a drop of rain called? _____ *a raindrop* _____

1. What is a case of books called? _____
2. What is a storm with thunder called? _____
3. What is a rocket in the sky called? _____
4. What is a dress worn in the sun called? _____
5. What is a house in a town called? _____
6. What is a flake of snow called? _____
7. What is the middle of the night called? _____
8. What is a pack for your back called? _____
9. What is a fighter of fires called? _____
10. What is the time for dinner called? _____

PRACTICE 59   Adverbs of Manner

ADJECTIVE	ADVERB	EXPLANATION
Steve was a **patient** teacher. He had a **quiet** voice. He had a **thoughtful** manner.	He taught **patiently.** He spoke **clearly.** He lived life **thoughtfully.**	We form most adverbs of manner by putting *–ly* at the end of an adjective.
This is a **fast** car. I have a **late** class. We had a **hard** test.	He drives **fast.** I arrived **late.** I studied **hard.**	Some adjectives and adverbs have the same form.
Susan was a **good** doctor.	She cared **well** for her patients.	This adverb is completely different from the adjective form..

LANGUAGE NOTES:

1. Adverbs of manner usually follow the verb phrase.

Subject	Verb phrase	Adverb
My friend	did his homework	quickly.

2. You can use *very* before an adverb of manner.
   She speaks *very* quickly.

EXERCISE 1   Fill in each blank with the correct form of the word in parentheses ( ).

Example: My friend reads (quick) _____ *quickly* _____.

1. I eat very (slow) _____.
2. My teacher speaks (clear) _____.
3. I try to write (neat) _____.
4. He plays the piano very (bad) _____.
5. She reads very (fast) _____.
6. George paints (beautiful) _____.
7. I slept very (deep) _____ last night.
8. They worked (hard) _____ on their project.
9. She dances so (wild) _____!
10. Could you speak more (quiet) _____ please?
11. They play the music very (loud) _____.
12. The children are playing (rough) _____.
13. You can come (late) _____ to the party if you want.
14. My husband cooks (good) _____.

15. You should read the instructions (careful) _____ .

16. We eat at this restaurant (frequent) _____ .

17. I try to live my life (creative) _____ .

18. We do our best to eat (healthy) _____ .

EXERCISE 2   Write a sentence to agree or disagree with the given statements.
If you want to make your adjective stronger, add *very*. You can use the
adjectives in the box below.

lightly / heavily or soundly	quietly / loudly	quickly or briskly or fast / slowly
late / early softly / hard	well / poorly or badly	neatly / messily
gracefully / clumsily		

Example: You write carefully. _No, I write quickly._

  or _Yes, I write **very** carefully._

1. You sleep lightly. _____

2. You eat slowly. _____

3. You walk briskly. _____

4. You cook well. _____

5. You draw well. _____

6. You read quickly. _____

7. You talk quietly. _____

8. You pronounce English well. _____

9. You laugh loudly. _____

10. You dance gracefully. _____

11. You dress neatly. _____

12. You shop quickly. _____

13. You study late. _____

14. You run slowly. _____

15. You write messily. _____

16. You type briskly. _____

PRACTICE 60 Spelling of –ly Adverbs

ADJECTIVE ENDING	EXAMPLE	ENDING	ADVERB
–*y*	easy	Change *y* to *i* and add –*ly*.	easi**ly**
	lucky		lucki**ly**
	happy		happi**ly**
consonant + *le*	simple	Drop the –*e* and add –*y*.	simp**ly**
	double		doub**ly**
	comfortable		comfortab**ly**
consonant + *e*	nice	Add –*ly*.	nice**ly**
	free		free**ly**
	brave		brave**ly**

LANGUAGE NOTE: There is one exception for the last rule: true-truly.

EXERCISE 1   Fill in each blank with the adverb form of the underlined adjective.

Example: This bed is so comfortable. I slept *comfortably*_____.

1.   This cake tastes wonderful. You bake _____.
2.   I'll always be true. I love you _____.
3.   What crazy kids! They play so _____.
4.   I try to stay healthy. I eat as _____ as I can.
5.   What a hearty meal! We ate _____.
6.   My car is so reliable. I can always trust it to run _____.
7.   His voice isn't clear. I wish he would speak _____.
8.   This is a reputable company. They are sure to do business _____.
9.   My room is messy. I do everything _____.
10. Don't be so hasty. You always act _____.
11. Your computer is unreliable. It seems to work _____.
12. I'm wearing a fancy dress. I'm dressed _____.
13. Her voice sounds so sweet. She sings so _____.
14. I like Betty, but she's irresponsible. She always behaves _____.
15. Mimi is a clever chess player. She plays _____.

EXERCISE 2 The adjective is in parentheses ( ). Use the adjective as it is, or change it to an adverb to fill in each blank.

Examples: You did (bad) _____*badly*_____ on the test.

Your composition was (good) _____*good*_____ this time.

Ms. Lee: Wendy, I'd like to talk to you about your class work. You're doing very (good)

(1) _____. You started a little (slow) (2) _____,

but you are learning more (quick) (3) _____ now.

Wendy: Thanks. English isn't so (difficult) (4) _____ for me now. And I try to

work (hard) (5) _____ on grammar.

Ms. Lee: About your skills: You listen (careful) (6) _____, and you speak

quite (fluent) (7) _____. However, you seem to read (careless)

(8) _____, and you need to write in your journal more (frequent)

(9) _____.

Wendy: Yes, I know. I don't like the book we are reading very much. It's not very (interesting)

(10) _____. And when we discuss the questions in groups,

the other students are (shy) (11) _____ and (quiet)

(12) _____. I don't like to be the only one speaking (loud)

(13) _____.

Ms. Lee: I know, but you are doing a (great) (14) _____ job. Keep up the

(good) (15) _____ work, Wendy.

PRACTICE 61 — Uses and Forms of *Too* versus *Very* and *Enough*

EXAMPLE	EXPLANATION
Mozart was **very** young when he learned to play the piano. The Egyptian pyramids are **very** old.	*Very* shows a large degree or extreme amount. It doesn't indicate any problems.
I am **too** poor. He is **too** sick **to work.**	*Too* shows that there is a problem. We often use an infinitive after *too* + adjective.
He is old **enough** to go to college. She has **enough** time **to review** her notes for class.	*Enough* shows that there is a sufficient amount (referring to the adjective). Infinitives also follow *enough*.

TOO + ADJECTIVE / ADVERB	ADVERB / ADJECTIVE + *ENOUGH*	*ENOUGH* + NOUN
My mother is 60. She's **too** young to retire.	My father is 65. He's old **enough** to retire.	He rides a bicycle every day. He gets **enough** exercise.
Bobby is **too** young to start school.	He is smart **enough** to be in third grade.	He has **enough** intelligence to read books for older children.
Ellen runs **too** quickly for me to catch up.	She runs quickly **enough** to be on the track team.	She has **enough** speed to win against other schools.
Level 5 is **too** hard for me.	This level is easy **enough** for me.	We have **enough** time to finish this lesson.

EXERCISE 1 Fill in each blank with *very* or *too*.

Examples: I'm _____*too*_____ short to touch the ceiling.

I'm _____*very*_____ happy to see you.

1. He is _____ big to wear this suit.

2. This book is _____ interesting.

3. It's _____ nice to meet you.

4. I am _____ hungry to concentrate.

5. It was _____ sweet of you to bring me flowers.

6. The World Trade Center is _____ tall.

7. She dances _____ gracefully.

8.   It's _____ hot outside today to be comfortable.

9.   I wake up _____ early every day.

10. He got there _____ late to see the film.

11. I'm _____ interested in butterflies.

12. I need a _____ small nail.

13. It's _____ crowded. He has so many things in his room.

14. I'm _____ old to go to discos.

15. That's a _____ strange car.

16. This chocolate is _____ delicious.

17. This ice cream is _____ sweet to eat.

18. They are _____ rich people.

19. It's _____ nice outside today.

20. I want a _____ cold glass of water.

EXERCISE 2 Fill in each blank with *too* plus the word in parentheses ( ) or with the word in parentheses plus *enough*.

Examples: I want to learn Chinese, but it's (difficult) _____*too difficult*_____ for me.

Four hours of studying is (studying) _____*enough studying*_____ for today.

1.   I can't eat candy. It's (sweet) _____ for me.

2.   I can't believe you wore a sweater! It's 95 degrees! It's (warm) _____ outside.

3.   I want a new computer, but I don't have (money) _____.

4.   Did you eat (food) _____ today?

5.   This bag is (heavy) _____ for me to carry.

6.   It's (cold) _____ today to leave the house.

7.   He's (handsome) _____ to be a movie star.

8.   They have (clothes) _____ to last all winter.

9.   I'm not (tired) _____ to go to sleep.

10. I'm (serious) _____ to laugh.

11. Could you heat up this soup? It isn't (hot) _____.

12. She's (proud) _____ to beg.

PRACTICE 62 Comparatives and Superlatives

EXAMPLE	EXPLANATION
New York City is the **biggest** city in the United States. California is the **most populated** state in the United States.	We use the superlative form of adjectives to point out the number 1 item in a group of three or more.
Los Angeles is bigger than Chicago. There are **more** people in California than in Peru.	We use the comparative form of adjectives to compare two items.

LANGUAGE NOTES:
1. Identify the superlative form by the word *most* + adjective or by the endings –st or –est.
2. Identify the regular comparative form by the word *more* + adjective or by the ending –er.

EXERCISE 1 Next to each comparative sentence, write a **2** to show that it compares two items (comparative). Next to each superlative sentence, write a **3+** to show that the item is the best of three or more.

Examples: That was definitely the best movie. _____3+_____

My handwriting is better than yours. _____2_____

1. He is the nicest person. _____
2. I have the worst eyesight. _____
3. This apartment is bigger than mine. _____
4. The oranges are sweeter. _____
5. This is the coldest day so far. _____
6. That painting is more beautiful than I remember. _____
7. Which one do you like better? _____
8. This is the most wonderful day of my life. _____
9. Today's test was easier than the last one. _____
10. I have the worst cold of my whole life. _____
11. I'm a bit shorter than my mother. _____
12. That was the most interesting painting at the museum. _____
13. I don't work now. I am poorer than last year. _____
14. This is the best school in the country. _____

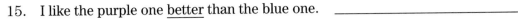
15. I like the purple one <u>better</u> than the blue one. _____

16. She works <u>harder</u> than anyone in the class. _____

17. She works <u>the hardest</u>. _____

18. That was the <u>funniest</u> joke! _____

19. He is <u>the most handsome</u> man I have ever seen. _____

20. He is even <u>more handsome</u> than my boyfriend. _____

EXERCISE 2   Fill in each blank with your opinion. Change *is* to *am* or *are* if necessary.

Examples: Ice cream is more delicious than *cake*_____ .

   *Orange soda*_ is the best drink.

1. Pizza is better than _____ .

2. School is more interesting than _____ .

3. _____ is my best friend.

4. _____ is my least favorite month.

5. Summertime is the most _____ .

6. A rose is more beautiful than _____ .

7. _____ is the funniest person I know.

8. English grammar is easier than _____ .

9. _____ is my easiest class.

10. My bedroom is smaller than _____ .

11. This city is more modern than _____ .

12. _____ is the most frightening movie I know.

13. _____ is the best food for a party.

14. _____ is the best drink for babies.

15. The beach is more relaxing than _____ .

PRACTICE 63 Comparative and Superlative Forms of Adjectives and Adverbs

	SIMPLE	COMPARATIVE	SUPERLATIVE
One-syllable adjectives and adverbs	tall	taller	the tallest
	fast	faster	the fastest
(Note spelling changes in words ending in C-V-C.)	sad	sadder	the saddest
	big	bigger	the biggest
Two-syllable adjectives that end in –*y*	easy	easier	the easiest
	happy	happier	the happiest
(Note spelling changes in words ending in –*y*.)			
Other two-syllable adjectives	frequent	more frequent	the most frequent
	active	more active	the most active
Some two-syllable adjectives have two forms	simple	simpler	the simplest
		more simple	the most simple
(Other two-syllable adjectives that have two forms are *handsome, quiet, gentle, narrow, clever, common, friendly, angry, polite, stupid.*)			
Adjectives with three or more syllables	important	more important	the most important
	difficult	more difficult	the most difficult
–*ly* adverbs	quickly	more quickly	the most quickly
Irregular adjectives / adverbs	good / well	better	the best
	bad / badly	worse	the worst
	far	farther	the farthest
	little	less	the least
	a lot	more	the most

LANGUAGE NOTE: *Bored* and *tired* are considered two-syllable adjectives and use *more* and *the most* in the comparative form.

I am *more tired* than you today.

I am *the most tired* of our whole team.

EXERCISE 1 Fill in the missing simple, comparative, or superlative adjective.

Example: cold _____*colder*_____ the coldest

1. good _____ the best

2. fast	_____	the fastest
3. polite	more polite	_____
4. _____	worse	the worst
5. busy	busier	_____
6. quiet	_____	the quietest
7. intelligent	_____	the most intelligent
8. lazy	lazier	_____
9. friendly	friendlier	_____
10. famous	_____	the most famous
11. ugly	_____	the ugliest
12. old	older	_____

EXERCISE 2 The underlined adjectives are incorrectly spelled. Rewrite the sentence with a correctly spelled adjective.

Example: She is <u>tallerer</u> than her sister.   *She is taller than her sister.*

1. This grammar homework is <u>importanter</u> than the reading homework.

   _____

2. He is <u>the bordest</u> of all the students.

   _____

3. That kind of bird is <u>more commoner</u> in Antarctica.

   _____

4. Math class is <u>easyer</u> for me than science class.

   _____

5. She is the <u>happyest</u> sister in the family.

   _____

6. My boss is <u>the tallerest</u> man in the company.

   _____

7. The person that helped me is <u>nicerer</u> than the person before him.

   _____

8. He is <u>the most activest</u> athlete at school.

   _____

9. She runs <u>more quicklier</u> than he runs.

   _____

10. He was <u>the sadest</u> when the teacher gave out the test scores.

   _____

PRACTICE 64 Superlatives and Word Order

EXAMPLE	EXPLANATION
Which country is **the largest?** Russia is **the largest** country.	Put superlative adjectives after the verb *be* or before the noun.
The Hispanic population is **growing the most quickly** in the United States.	Put superlative adverbs after the verb phrase.
It snows **the most** in Alaska.	Put *the most, the least, the best,* or *the worst* after a verb.
The desert gets **the most** sunshine.	Put *the most, the least, the best,* or *the worst* before a noun.

LANGUAGE NOTES:

1. We sometimes put a prepositional phrase at the end of a superlative sentence:

    He is the fastest long-distance runner *in the Olympics.*

2. We often say "one of the" before a superlative form. Then we use a plural noun:

    She is *one of the* nicest *students.*

    That guy is *one of the* smartest *people.*

EXERCISE 1 Add the expression to the sentence. Change the nouns and verbs in the sentence as needed. Change the order as needed.

Examples: (the most)   He smiles in class.   *He smiles the most in class.*

(one of the)   She is a nice person.   *She is one of the nicest people.*

1. (one of the smallest)   Liechtenstein is a country.

_____

2. (the least)   My city gets sunshine in the winter.

_____

3. (one of the)   My computer teacher is friendly.

_____

4. (the most quickly)   She always finishes her work.

_____

5. (the least quickly)   Of the whole class, I finished.

_____

6. (the worst)   Disease and poverty are problems in the world.

_____

7. (the most)   My mother laughs in my family.

_____

EXERCISE 2   Write a sentence about the first person you can think of for each of these adjectives.

Example: rich   _The richest person I can think of is Bill Gates._ _____

1. interesting   _____
2. gentle   _____
3. talented   _____
4. reliable   _____
5. powerful   _____

EXERCISE 3   Write a sentence about someone in your class who is the superlative in each of the following activities.

Example: listens well   _Monica listens the best in my class._ _____

1. takes good notes   _____
2. listens well   _____
3. asks a lot of questions   _____
4. pronounces English well   _____
5. comes to class late   _____

EXERCISE 4   Write a superlative sentence, giving your opinion about each of the following items.

Example: good flavor of ice cream   _The best flavor of ice cream is chocolate._

1. good season   _____
2. delicious fruit   _____
3. beautiful color   _____
4. good song   _____
5. good sport   _____

PRACTICE 65 Comparisons

EXAMPLE	EXPLANATION
Brazil is *bigger than* Japan. Los Angeles is *more expensive than* Mexico City.	We use the comparative form to compare two items. We use *than* before the second item of comparison.

LANGUAGE NOTES:

1. Omit *than* if the second item of comparison is not included:
   Tahiti is *warmer*.
2. *Much* or *a little* can come before a comparative form:
   Your handbag was *much* more expensive than my backpack.
3. Use subject pronouns or possessive pronouns after *than*.
   Conversational English uses object pronouns. That is considered informal English:
   She is taller than *I*. (formal)
   She is taller than *me*. (informal)
   Her hair is curlier than *mine*.

EXERCISE 1 Unscramble the following words to make sentences of comparison.

Example: has / than / darker / me / hair / she   *She has darker hair than I.*

1. he / taller / is / much / you / than

   _____

2. his / your / eyes / little / a / are / than / lighter

   _____

3. hair / mother's / is / mine / a little / my / than / longer

   _____

4. much / she / more tired / is / you / than

   _____

5. are / legs / a little / your / longer / hers / than

   _____

EXERCISE 2 Write sentences comparing public transportation (trains, buses, etc.) and cars. Give your own opinion.

Example: (cars / trains / convenient)   *Cars are more convenient than trains.*

1. (sailboats / cars / good for the environment)

   _____

2. (train / bus / cheap)

_____

3. (airplane / bus / expensive)

_____

4. (airplane / train / enjoyable)

_____

5. (train / bus / good for long trips)

_____

6. (bicycle / train / good for short trips)

_____

7. (airplane / car / safe)

_____

8. (bicycle / car / clean)

_____

9. (bicycle / motorcycle / dangerous)

_____

10. (boat / airplane / fast)

_____

EXERCISE 3   Write sentences comparing one of your former schools and your present school. Give your own opinion.

Example: fun   _My former teachers were more fun than the teachers now._

1. new _____
2. friendly _____
3. large _____
4. noisy _____
5. clean _____
6. disciplined _____

EXAMPLE	EXPLANATION
Houses in the north are **more expensive** than houses in the south.	Put comparative adjectives after the verb *be*.
I want to move to a **warmer** climate.	Put comparative adjectives before a noun.
He found a job **more quickly** in Rome.	Put comparative adverbs after the verb phrase.
She speaks English **more fluently** than I do.	It rains **more** in Ireland.
You drive **better** than I.	Put *more, less, better,* or *worse* after a verb.
Ireland has **more** rain than Spain.	Put *more, less, fewer, better,* or *worse* before a noun.
Ireland has **less** sun than Spain.	
LANGUAGE NOTE: Use *than* before the second item in a comparison.	

EXERCISE 1 Unscramble the words to make good statements of comparison. The subject of the sentence is the first word or pronoun.

Example: I / my friend / more / dress / casually / than

I dress more casually than my friend.

1. She / quickly / less / eats / her / children / than

    _____

2. The tutor / better / than / writes / students / his

    _____

3. You / your / laugh / frequently / sister / than / less

    _____

4. The sky here / clearer / than / my / is / in / city

    _____

5. Children / more / than / teenagers / walk / slowly

    _____

6. My mother / fashionable / more / I / than / is

    _____

7. There / insects / are / at night / fewer / than / in Florida / here

    _____

8. That car / expensive / than / my / is / car / more

    _____

9. His temper / worse / father's / my / temper / is / than

_____

10. They / than / slowly / more / speak / we

_____

EXERCISE 2 Put the following words in the correct position in the sentence.

Example: better / I play tennis than my mother.

I play tennis better than my mother. _____

1. emptier / That garbage can is than that one.

_____

2. older / Your television is than mine.

_____

3. faster / His garden grew than ours.

_____

4. noisier / You always have parties than we.

_____

5. less beautiful / That painting is than this one.

_____

6. more safely / We drive a car than that driver.

_____

7. worse / She sings than her sister.

_____

8. fewer / People in the country have health problems than people in the city.

_____

9. worse / I have health than my brother Joe.

_____

10. better / Joe has health care than I.

_____

AFFIRMATIVE STATEMENT

A soccer team has 11 players,	and a football team **does too.**
My brother plays soccer,	and I **do too.**
Baseball is popular in the United States,	and basketball **is too.**
I like baseball.	I **do too.**
I liked basketball last year.	You did too.
I will go to a game next month.	You will too.

NEGATIVE STATEMENT

Football **isn't** popular in my country,	and baseball **isn't either.**
I **don't** like football.	My brother **doesn't either.**
He **can't** play tennis well.	I **can't either.**
He couldn't play baseball well.	I couldn't either.
He won't play tennis well.	I won't either.

LANGUAGE NOTES:

1. The auxiliary verbs are *do, does, did,* the modals (*can, will,* etc.), and *be.* We use auxiliary verbs in the above sentences to avoid repetitions of the same verb phrase.
2. Use *too* with two affirmative statements. Use *either* with two negative statements. We can connect the sentences with *and.*

EXERCISE 1 Underline the verb in the first part of the sentence. Circle the correct answer to finish each affirmative statement with an auxiliary verb.

Examples: Judy <u>likes</u> animals, and Mary did too /(does too.)

Steve <u>will</u> pass the test, and you (will too)/ do too.

1. Judy can play the guitar, and Mary <u>can too / does too.</u>

2. Judy has a new hat, and Mary <u>do too / does too.</u>

3. Judy is 12 years old, and Mary <u>is too / does too.</u>

4. I had a cold last week, and she <u>did too / does too.</u>

5. She watched a lot of TV, and I <u>does too / did too.</u>

6. She will eat chicken for dinner tonight, and I <u>can too / will too.</u>

7. He wants a new pair of jeans, and they <u>do too / does too.</u>

8. They will buy a pizza, and he <u>does too / will too.</u>

9. Judy may go shopping tomorrow, and he <u>might too / does too.</u>

10. Judy might be a doctor when she grows up, and they <u>can too / might too</u>.

11. Judy could read when she was three years old, and you <u>can too / could too</u>.

12. Judy can speak two languages, and you <u>do too / can too</u>.

13. Judy saw a movie yesterday, and we <u>do too / did too</u>.

14. Judy was sleepy last night, and we <u>does / were too</u>.

15. My sister does her homework every day, and I <u>can too / do too</u>.

16. I am hungry, and they <u>do too / are too</u>.

17. You will be sleepy, and I <u>will be too / am too</u>.

18. We are going there, and he <u>are too / is too</u>.

19. She does her laundry, and he <u>does his too / does its too</u>.

20. They did well on the test, and you <u>do too / did too</u>.

EXERCISE 2 Underline the negative verb in each sentence. Finish each negative statement with an auxiliary verb of the same tense + *either*.

Example: Judy <u>doesn't like</u> green peppers, and Mary *doesn't either* .

1. Judy isn't very tall, and Mary _____.

2. Judy doesn't play the piano, and Mary _____.

3. Judy can't stand on her head, and Mary _____.

4. Judy won't eat bananas, and Mary _____.

5. Judy didn't study French yesterday, and Mary _____.

6. Judy wouldn't like to rent a horror video, and Mary _____.

7. Judy isn't bored, and Mary _____.

8. Judy may not watch TV tonight, and Mary _____.

9. Judy didn't wash the dishes yet, and Mary _____.

10. Judy can't stand tomatoes, and Mary _____.

11. Judy doesn't have a cold now, and Mary _____.

12. Judy won't call her friend today, and Mary _____.

13. Judy couldn't go to the movies last Friday, and Mary _____.

14. Judy didn't have a birthday yesterday, and Mary _____.

15. Judy isn't lonely, and Mary _____.

PRACTICE 68 Auxiliary Verbs with Opposite Statements

AFFIRMATIVE	NEGATIVE
I like football,	but my brother **doesn't.**
Football is popular in my country,	but baseball **isn't.**

NEGATIVE	AFFIRMATIVE
You didn't see the soccer game,	but I **did.**
Football players can't carry the ball,	but soccer players **can.**

EXERCISE 1 People are different in some ways. Underline the verb in the first part of the sentence. Then circle the correct answer to complete the sentence with opposite statements in the same verb tense.

Example: Judy likes cats, but Mary (doesn't) / isn't.

1. Judy is good at math, but Mary isn't / doesn't.
2. Judy doesn't like cooking, but Mary does / doesn't.
3. Judy doesn't have a backpack, but Mary does / isn't.
4. Judy will eat spinach, but Mary doesn't / won't.
5. Judy can swim fast, but Mary can / can't.
6. He didn't go to the library, but she didn't / did.
7. She can't spell very well, but he can / can't.
8. She wasn't good at skating, but he was / is.
9. He has a lot of magazines, but she does / doesn't.
10. He wrote a story, but she wasn't / didn't.
11. They won't make sandwiches, but I will / won't.
12. They can speak French, but I can / can't.
13. We eat a lot, but they doesn't / don't.
14. We are interested in butterflies, but he aren't / isn't.
15. I will go to college, but you aren't / won't.
16. I went on a picnic last weekend, but you aren't / didn't.
17. She likes to watch comedies, but he doesn't / wasn't.
18. She can't run fast, but he does / can.
19. He was tired yesterday, but his friend won't / wasn't.
20. Judy's room is big, but Mary's doesn't / isn't.

Compare the two places or things enclosed in parentheses. Use *but* for differences. Use an auxiliary verb in all cases.

Example: (your brother / my brother)

Your brother paints houses, but my brother doesn't _____ .

(my English teacher / other teachers)

My English teacher rides a bicycle to school, but the other teachers don't ___ .

1. (my family / your family)

   _____ , but _____ .

2. (my present teacher / my former teacher)

   _____ , but _____ .

3. (my friends / your friends)

   _____ , but _____ .

4. (my English pronunciation / your English pronunciation)

   _____ , but _____ .

5. (baseball / basketball)

   _____ , but _____ .

6. (pizza / rice)

   _____ , but _____ .

7. (cats / dogs)

   _____ , but _____ .

8. (the weather here / the weather at home)

   _____ , but _____ .

9. (ice cream / candy)

   _____ , but _____ .

10. (large cars / small cars)

   _____ , but _____ .

Auxillary Verbs with Opposite Statements

PRACTICE **69** Auxiliary Verbs in Tag Questions

AFFIRMATIVE STATEMENT	NEGATIVE TAG QUESTION	ANSWER
A football team has 11 players,	**doesn't** it?	Yes, it does.
You can play football,	**can't** you?	Yes, I can.
This is your football.	**isn't** it?	Yes, it is.
There are 11 players on a baseball team	**aren't** there?	No, there aren't.

NEGATIVE STATEMENT	AFFIRMATIVE TAG QUESTION	ANSWER
Soccer isn't the same as football,	**is** it?	No, it isn't.
Football players don't wear a helmet,	**do** they?	Yes, they do.
Soccer players can't carry the ball,	**can** they?	No, they can't.
I'm right,	**aren't** I?	Yes, you are.

LANGUAGE NOTES:

1. A tag question is a short question that we put at the end of a statement. Use a tag question to ask if your statement is correct or if the listener agrees with you.
2. A tag question uses the auxiliary verb + a subject pronoun.
3. The tag question uses the same tense as the main verb.
4. An affirmative question uses a negative tag. A negative statement uses an affirmative tag.
5. *Am I not* is a very formal tag. We usually say, *aren't I?*
6. When *have* is the main verb, American English usually uses *do, does,* or *did* in the tag question.
    You *have tickets to the game,* don't you?

EXERCISE 1 Match the correct tag question to each affirmative statement.

Example: This is a new restaurant, _d. isn't it?_

1. You're a new waiter, _____   a. aren't I?
2. You can order fish here, _____   b. isn't there?
3. You will bring us some more bread, _____   c. wouldn't you?
4. He should bring us some water, _____   d. isn't it?
5. There are restrooms in this restaurant, _____   e. won't you?
6. You'd like to order now, _____   f. can't you?
7. This is a delicious dish, _____   g. aren't you?
8. I'm ordering too much food, _____   h. aren't there?

9. There is free parking here, _____   i. wasn't it?

10. This was a lovely meal, _____   j. shouldn't he?

EXERCISE **2**   Circle the correct tag question for each of these negative statements.

Example: You aren't Robert, (are you) / aren't you?

1. Today isn't Monday, <u>was it / is it</u>?

2. You aren't working now, <u>are we / are you</u>?

3. I can't sleep here, <u>can't I / can I</u>?

4. We shouldn't take photos here, <u>should we / do we</u>?

5. These glasses aren't yours, <u>are they / aren't they</u>?

6. You weren't sick last week, <u>was you / were you</u>?

7. There aren't any mosquitoes here, <u>aren't there / are there</u>?

8. This shop is expensive, <u>isn't that / isn't it</u>?

9. Those aren't your gloves, <u>are there / are they</u>?

10. You won't forget this, <u>won't you / will you</u>?

EXERCISE **3**   Add a tag question to these affirmative and negative statements.

Examples: He speaks a lot of languages, *doesn't he?* _____

He isn't a mechanic, *is he?* _____

1. You have a lot of shoes, _____

2. I don't have the textbook, _____

3. He wants to go to Florida, _____

4. You didn't go to work today, _____

5. We don't always use this room, _____

6. She understands Russian, _____

7. Your uncle didn't come to the play, _____

8. We had a big problem yesterday _____

9. Your mother doesn't make your lunch, _____

10. Your father doesn't like sports, _____

11. The alphabet has 26 letters, _____

12. They went to Indonesia last month, _____

PRACTICE 70 Answering a Tag Question

RIGHT INFORMATION	AGREEMENT
Italy is in Europe, isn't it?	**Yes, it is.**
Belgium isn't a city, is it?	**No, it isn't.** It's a country.

WRONG INFORMATION	DISAGREEMENT OR CORRECTION
Russia isn't a big country, is it?	**Yes, it is.** It's very big.
San Francisco is a big city, isn't it?	**No, it isn't.** It's small.

LANGUAGE NOTES:
1. When we use a tag question, we normally ask the listener to agree with us.
2. When we add a negative tag question, we expect the answer to be *yes*.
   No means the information is incorrect or the listener does not agree.
3. When we add an affirmative tag question, we expect the answer to be *no*.
   Yes means the information is incorrect or the listener does not agree.

EXERCISE 1 For each of the following questions, write a short answer according to the response given.

Examples: You're studying English, aren't you? (yes) *Yes, I am.*

We liked playing soccer, didn't we? (no) *No, we didn't.*

1. We have a big family, don't we? (yes) _____
2. You don't like TV, do you? (no) _____
3. He can sing beautifully, can't he? (yes) _____
4. She went to another country last year, didn't she? (yes) _____
5. You will continue studying English, won't you? (no) _____
6. They have a car, don't they? (yes) _____
7. You aren't happy, are you? (no) _____
8. There are some pets at your house, aren't there? (no) _____
9. Your father speaks English very well, doesn't he? (yes) _____
10. That computer is a great tool, isn't it? (yes) _____
11. There are three kittens in the basket, aren't there? (no) _____
12. I have two more math problems, don't I? (no) _____
13. They will meet all our friends, won't they? (yes) _____
14. We weren't happy in elementary school, were we? (no) _____
15. Our bus left at one o'clock, didn't it? (yes) _____

EXERCISE 2 Complete the tag question in the left column. Then check the meaning of the answer in the right column.

Example:

    A. You aren't tired, are you?   Person B is tired.

    B. No, *I'm not*   .   ✔ Person B isn't tired.

1. **A.** You don't have any change, do you?   Person B has change.

    B. No, _____.   Person B doesn't have change.

2. **A.** You don't like studying, do you?   Person B likes studying.

    B. Yes, _____.   Person B doesn't like studying.

3. **A.** Pink is the most beautiful color, isn't it?   Person B agrees with the statement.

    B. No, _____.   Person B doesn't agree with the statement.

4. **A.** You don't know what time it is, do you?   Person B knows what time it is.

    B. No, _____.   Person B doesn't know what time it is.

5. **A.** You go to school every day, don't you?   Person B goes to school every day.

    B. Yes, _____.   Person B doesn't go to school every day.

6. **A.** You don't have any time now, do you?   Person B has time now.

    B. No, _____.   Person B doesn't have any time now.

7. **A.** You are Mary's sister, aren't you?   Person B is Mary's sister.

    B. Yes, _____.   Person B isn't Mary's sister.

8. **A.** You have a lot of books, don't you?   Person B has a lot of books.

    B. No, _____.   Person B doesn't have a lot of books.

EXERCISE 3 Answer each question with your own opinion. If you give a *no* answer, explain why you think this way.

Examples: Your apartment is small, isn't it?   *No, it isn't. It's very large.*

                 You love swimming, don't you?   *Yes, I do.*

1. Your family lives near this school, don't they? _____

2. You don't study in the library every day, do you? _____

3. You love all sports, don't you _____

4. Your best friend is a laywer, isn't she / he? _____

HEINLE & HEINLE

THOMSON LEARNING

More Grammar Practice 1

Vice President, Editorial Director ESL: *Nancy Leonhardt*
Senior Production Editor: *Michael Burggren*
Acquisitions Editor: *Eric Bredenberg*
Associate Developmental Editor: *Sarah Barnicle*
Marketing Manager: *Charlotte Sturdy*
Manufacturing Coordinator: *Mary Beth Hennebury*

Contributing Writer: *Nada Gordon*
Composition/Project Management: *Ecomlinks, Inc.*
Cover/Text Design: *Linda Dana Willis*
Printer: *Courier*

For more information contact Heinle & Heinle, 20 Park Plaza, Boston, Massachusetts 02116 USA, or you can visit our Internet site at http://www.heinle.com

For permission to use material from this text or product contact us:
Tel   1-800-730-2214
Fax   1-800-730-2215
Web   www.thomsonrights.com

ISBN: 0-8384-1893-7

International Division List

ASIA (excluding India)
Thomson Learning
60 Albert Street #15-01
Albert Complex
Singapore 189969

AUSTRALIA/NEW ZEALAND
Nelson/Thomson Learning
102 Dodds Street
South Melbourne
Victoria 3205 Australia

CANADA
Nelson/Thomson Learning
1120 Birchmount Road
Scarborough, Ontario
Canada M1K 5G4

LATIN AMERICA
Thomson Learning
Seneca, 53
Colonia Polanco
11560 México D.F. México

SPAIN
Thomson Learning
Calle Magallanes, 25
28015-Madrid
Espana

UK/EUROPE/MIDDLE EAST
Thomson Learning
Berkshire House
168-173 High Holborn
London, WC1V 7AA, United Kingdom